Mainly on Directing

Mainly on Directing

Gypsy, West Side Story, and Other Musicals

Arthur Laurents

Alfred A. Knopf · New York
2009

THIS IS A BORZOI BOOK
PUBLISHED BY ALFRED A. KNOPF

Knopf, Borzoi Books, and the colophon are
registered trademarks of Random House, Inc.

Library of Congress Cataloging-in-Publication Data
Laurents, Arthur.
Mainly on directing : Gypsy, West Side Story, and other musicals / by Arthur
Laurents. —1st ed.
p.   cm.
"A Borzoi book."
ISBN 978-0-307-27088-7
1. Musicals—Production and direction.   2. Laurents, Arthur.   3. Styne, Jule,
1905–1994. Gypsy.   4. Bernstein, Leonard, 1918–1990. West Side Story.   I. Title.
ML1711.5.L38 2009
792.602'33092—dc22   2008055541

Manufactured in the United States of America
First Edition

*To David Saint and
his George Street Playhouse*

Mainly on Directing

ONE

In the Bones

"THE SHOW DEPENDS ON YOU," Scott Rudin said. "You have the musical in your bones; Sam doesn't. You have to put it there for him."

The remark wasn't meant to be either flattering or challenging; it was simply Scott stating my task for his upcoming revival of *Gypsy* in 2003. With Bernadette Peters as a very different Rose, the production, though headed for New York, was to originate in London. Thus it had an English co-producer, Robert Fox, and an English director, very hot at that moment—Sam Mendes. What I didn't realize then was that the remark wasn't simply a Scott Rudinism; it was an acute perception of what could be an Achilles' heel. By the time I did realize that, Scott was gone, the production had been shifted to originate in New York, and no one in charge really knew much about Broadway musicals, including the director to whom all bowed. No musical, no matter how good, can survive a misdirected, misconceived production, and this one was no exception.

There had been two major revivals of *Gypsy* in New York: one with Angela Lansbury in 1974, the other with Tyne Daly in 1989. *Gypsy* takes its tone and style from the actress playing Rose: Merman, a legend in the original, Angie and Tyne, each brilliant in her own way, in the two I had directed. I wanted someone else to direct this one because I wanted to see what that someone else would do; I hoped to be surprised. "Surprised" was not the word for my reaction to what Sam Mendes did. "Surprised" is a happy word.

He was Scott's suggestion, enthusiastically endorsed by his friend Robert Fox. Robert was as good-looking as his better-known actor brothers, James and Edward, but actors are seen more, so known more, than producers. He had taste, an executioner's tongue, a bucket of charm, and three ex-wives. He was not given to unconsidered enthusiasm or much ambition. Sam, who wasn't short on charm himself when necessary, had called me some years earlier about doing *Gypsy* at the Donmar Warehouse, the pocket-size theatre in London where he made his name. I thought the Donmar was too small. A year or so passed and Sam called again to offer a bigger venue: a West End legitimate theatre. Still too small for me. When London was dropped for the Bernadette Peters revival, one of the reasons given was Sam's feeling that the show was "a big Broadway musical."

I was eager to do *Gypsy* in London because it hadn't been seen in the West End since 1973, when the Angela Lansbury production premiered. Very heady, the reception was, from the opening night to the end of Angie's run. I wanted to repeat that dreamlike triumph thirty years later with Bernadette; but London, alas, was finessed. The reason given was that it would be too expensive to bring the production to New York. That was also given as the reason for not taking the production to Washington before opening in New York. Money is well regarded as a believable reason for not doing anything, but I checked to find out how much had been lost taking *Annie Get Your Gun* with Bernadette to Washington before it opened in New York. It had *made* $750,000. Who didn't want to take *Gypsy* to Washington? Not Scott; he, too, had been finessed. Not by the Brits, though—by Stephen Sondheim, because of another musical.

Called *Wise Guys,* this one opened at the New York Theatre Workshop not too long before *Gypsy* was scheduled to go into production in London. Involved in both shows were the same three major names: Steve, Scott, and Sam. There was probably an omen in that all three names begin with *S,* but no one was into anything as realistic as omens. *Wise Guys* (later retitled *Bounce* and, more recently, *Road Show*) was written by Steve (with John Weidman), produced by Scott, and directed by Sam. Each of the Three S's must have been aware that the show wasn't ready for a public outing: its second act was unfinished and its director had come straight from editing his first film *(American Beauty)* without time to digest the material. Why they went ahead, then, is a mystery only to those who have never done a musical. The brightest, the most experienced, the most talented makers of musicals, particularly the most talented, also believe they can walk on water.

The show's failure produced more schadenfreude than any in years; the apportioning of blame afterwards was inevitable. There is a touch of irony in that it was Scott, he who had promoted Sam for *Gypsy* and opposed him for *Wise Guys,* who got the heave-ho. He and Steve had a feud which grew so fierce and public that Steve refused to have Scott on *Gypsy.* Steve was the best lyricist and collaborator I had ever worked with. That refusal was his prerogative. Steve also demanded that as his friend, I stop speaking to Scott. That was *not* his prerogative. I refused; he said he and I couldn't be friends; he stopped speaking to me—which was greeted in the theatre community with "Oh, not again." But this is about *Gypsy,* not about Steve and me.

With London out and New York in, one would have thought Scott, an experienced New York producer, more essential than ever, and he was. With musicals, however, neither logic nor common sense prevails. By the time production was underway in New York, Robert Fox was odd man in. Noted for productions of classy plays in London (principally with Maggie Smith) and almost a neophyte when it came to musicals, Robert had replaced Scott with an American producer who *was* a neophyte: not only had he never produced a musical, he knew nothing about musicals. He was, however, a fan, an Anglophile, and he had a lot of lolly. After the first preview it was evident to everyone except Robert and his co-producer that this revival was in what is colloquially known as deep shit. My longtime partner, Tom Hatcher, came striding up the aisle as soon as the curtain came down and broke the news to Robert. Startled at first because Tom came from Tulsa, Oklahoma, and deceptively looked it, Robert recovered quickly, and his experienced tongue got to work. Too easily upset on my behalf, Tom struck back, and they played a juicy little scene at the back of the orchestra. A theatre gossip columnist standing nearby reported the episode the next day, except that in his version the argument was between Robert and me. That might have upset me in the days before *Nick and Nora,* when the *New York Times,* in a futile effort to increase circulation, had its own theatre gossip columnist who destroyed me every Friday during our endless previews. Like the show, she didn't last.

As the credited producer, Robert put all his chips on Sam; he believed Sam *did* walk on water, as indeed he had at his reservoir, the Donmar. But this was Broadway, this was the Shubert Theatre, and unlike Scott, Robert didn't know what it meant to have the musical in your bones. Thus he couldn't see that it wasn't in Sam's or understand why it needed to be.

What does it mean, the musical wasn't "in his bones"? For that matter, what exactly does "in the bones" mean? Well, there is no exact definition: the expression encompasses a feeling for the rhythm of the musical as a whole as well as of the scenes and numbers within it, for why and when and how to highlight a moment and make it musical without actual song or dance, for how and when to implant the emotional reality that makes a performance musical theatre, not musical comedy. It's not a skill, it can't be acquired with experience, it can't be learned or taught or injected—it's an instinct. Even excellent singers and dancers don't make excellent musical theatre performers if, despite their gifts, despite their technique, despite all their experience, the musical isn't in their bones. In Rose's words: "You either got it or you ain't." Unfortunately for Sam Mendes, his first directorial touch on *Gypsy* showed he didn't got it.

Gypsy starts before the director does, with that legendary, thrilling Jule Styne overture. Play the opening "I had a dream" chords (the show was a few years before Martin Luther King's historic speech) and the audience applauds as though cards have been held up in a television studio; it erupts over the trumpet solo in the burlesque section and roars its approval with the final orchestral flourish. It's flying on a musical high when the curtain rises on a noisy, brightly lit, garishly costumed rehearsal for *Uncle Jocko's Kiddie Show, Seattle*—as the illuminated signs say on either side of the vaudeville proscenium. During the brief scene, laughter comes fairly easily, because the audience is so exhilarated but also because it knows in its musical bones that something is coming that is going to send it even higher. And something does. Strutting down the aisle in all her vulgar glory is Rose. "Sing out, Louise!" she calls, and the roof of the theatre is knocked off. *Gypsy* is launched.

The rhythm and knowing drive to that opening beat were absent from the Mendes production. The overture worked its magic; the exhilarated audience was flying high; and then the curtain rose—on gloomy silence and the empty, cavernous stage of a dingy old theatre. Across the back wall, the designer added redundancy with one word in large, faded letters: SILENCE. A stooped, scraggy stagehand dragged himself out of the upstage shadows to cross oh-so-slowly downstage with placards to be inserted in the downstage light boxes. Before he had trudged halfway there, the audience had been lost. It had come down from its high and was ready for *The Iceman Cometh*. By the time Bernadette as Rose strutted down the aisle shouting "Sing out, Louise!" *Gypsy's* battery had died and she had to jump-start the show again all by herself.

The first five minutes of a musical are crucial: either the audience can be captured, in which case they are the director's, no matter what he or she does, until at least halfway through the first act; or they can be lost, in which case it will take some stage magic to get them back before the end of the first act, if ever. Never mind intelligence and craft, never mind desire, never mind talent. If the musical were in your bones, you would never follow that dazzling overture with the gloomy silence of an empty, cavernous hole and the long wait while an old stagehand trudged across a dreary stage.

Nor would you have continued to show it wasn't in your bones right up to the big climactic eleven o'clock number, "Rose's Turn." For a director born for musicals, "Rose's Turn" is New Year's Eve in Times Square. It's his world and his stage on which to let his star loose theatrically. And legitimately, for the number takes place, not in reality, but in Rose's head, where she is "better than any of you!"—the greatest performer in the world, the star she had always wanted to be, hailed by wildly cheering fans. Raunchy, funny, sexy, vulgar, and underneath, always raging, always eaten up with hunger for the star she has never had on her door. She almost gets tripped up: there's a shaking passage where she questions herself. But she's Rose, and Rose doesn't give in or up: that eternal anger fuels her to insist on triumph, and triumph she does. The cheers in her head are louder than anyone ever heard in life.

Bernadette Peters's life in the theatre had made her more than ready. But that wasn't how Sam saw the number. Under his direction, "Rose's Turn" seemed to be "Bernadette Peters in Concert." Except for a rather dainty pass at a stripper's walk, she scarcely moved at all.

A director sometimes has a vision, a conception that he comes to from some place within himself. That it is at odds with the material he is directing doesn't seem to matter or even occur to him. The material—this is so elementary it shouldn't have to be stated, but almost every musical production in recent years seems oblivious to it—the material is the source for everything seen or said or done on the stage. The director, the choreographer, the designer, the actor who thinks he or she doesn't have to observe this is digging his own shallow grave.

A number like "Rose's Turn" is so strongly written, and Bernadette Peters is so strong a performer, that the audience applauded and cheered even though it wasn't getting full value: the star wasn't delivering that landmark number as brilliantly in her own original style as she undoubtedly could. Those who had seen the show before were well aware of this (New York overflows with musical-comedy queens who know every word of *Gypsy* and don't hesitate to voice their displeasure); those, like Sam, who had never seen the show weren't aware of what they were missing. The vehemence of the response the number gets anyway made it hard for Sam to see he had made a mistake—doubly hard when the producers, who also hadn't seen the show before, were functioning only as the director's faithful fans. Of course, all of them could have seen the video recording of the Tyne Daly revival at the Lincoln Center archives. (Actually, one of them did. Apparently he wasn't impressed.)

Bernadette Peters grew up in the theatre: she was a Hollywood Blonde in a touring company of *Gypsy* when she was eleven years old. When the company played a cut version in Las Vegas, I directed the show for the first time, and I must have directed Bernadette—as I wish I had when we were both back in our hometown and slightly older.

Bernadette has long been a total professional, beloved by every company she has graced. She has also long been a star, but she doesn't indulge in the conventional star behavior. That's admirable, but there are times when she has done herself and the show she is starring in a disservice by not taking advantage of her status. *Gypsy* was a glaring example. What she could really do, not only with "Rose's Turn" but with Rose herself, only became clear late in the run, when she finally asserted herself and let the lid off the performance that had been bottled up. Her "Everything's Coming Up

Roses" at the end of the first act brought both cheers and tears. Her whole, stunning performance galvanized the actors capable of letting loose with her. It might have brought the show to life, but too many in the company either had nothing to let loose or, like the over-the-top strippers, were bloated from scenery chewing. Bernadette's Rose did take its rightful place, but too late, and unseen by too many who should have seen it.

Sam tried hard to satisfy many of the notes I gave him, but my continued insistence that "Rose's Turn" was misconceived was hardest for him to accept: perhaps because he was deceived by the audience's response, perhaps because he liked to stage any musical number that didn't require real dancing himself and didn't want to entrust the number to the choreographer, Jerry Mitchell. Jerry, a gypsy through and through, had the musical in his bones. He had an undoable assignment: to embellish and improve on Jerry Robbins's original numbers. On his own, he staged the most audience-effective number in the whole show: Gypsy's final strip, done by Tammy Blanchard's incandescent Louise. That strip, however, was Las Vegas in Nevada, not Minsky on Forty-second Street. If the production had had any period authenticity, the staging would have seemed out of time and place and the number wouldn't have worked as well as it did. But the designer didn't have a sense of time, place, or period, so Jerry Mitchell provided a glitter and vitality that were a welcome relief from the brown quasi-earthiness that burdened the evening. He replicated the Robbins steps for "You Gotta Get a Gimmick" as best he could, but the number was massacred by the three shameless hamsters. Once again, the producers were deceived by the preview audience's response.

With "Rose's Turn," my notes had better luck. Just before the end of previews, Sam allowed Bernadette some freedom. That he did so was because Sam is essentially a literary man and finally saw the contradiction between the words Rose spoke and sang and her limited movement. Directors of plays usually don't give the same weight to the text when directing musicals. Music seduces.

For a long time now, it's been the rare musical that shows awareness of the vital importance of scenery, costumes, and lighting—the *look.* Shows like *Follies* and *La Cage aux Folles* seem relegated to nostalgia. The look in recent years usually seems to confuse mechanized vulgarity with theatricality. And the audience wonders (or at least *I* wonder): what happened to taste, to color sense, to visual style?

The responsibility is the director's, for in the end, the look of the musical is the director's look. He chooses the designers, he conveys his vision, he guides and edits. He can inspire the best to be even better or he can hamstring them into being less. For lighting his revival of *Gypsy,* Sam Mendes chose Jules Fisher and Peggy Eisenhauer, candidates for finest lighting designers in the country. Following the rules for being complete professionals, they put aside their knowledge, experience, and the musical instinct in their bones and did their best to satisfy the captain of their dark brown ship. For scenery and costumes, Sam chose his London colleague Anthony Ward. When we met, I remarked that *Gypsy* was very American. "What does that mean?" Ward sniffed. That he never bothered to find out was clear from his scenery; that he didn't even bother to find out who Rose was was clear from his dowdy costumes for Bernadette. Whatever Anthony Ward had in his bones, it wasn't musical or authenticity. There are still Brits who think we are their colonials.

The scenery for *Gypsy,* like the scenery for all Donmar productions, had no walls. This makes sense at the Donmar Warehouse in London, where walls would block the audience from seeing what's going on. It made no sense at the Shubert Theatre on Broadway in New York, because there was no clear reason why there weren't walls. The absence of walls in any set that was supposed to be a room left the audience unsure where a scene was taking place—in a kitchen, for example. The lack of walls wouldn't have mattered if the pieces that made up the set had been carefully chosen to convey "kitchen." Instead, all the rooms were composed of the same brown doorways, brown chairs, and brown table, all pushed around the stage by actors and/or stagehands in meticulously choreographed moves to music. The arrangement of doorways, chairs, and table changed for each scene, but the end result was always brown doorways, chairs, and table in an unidentifiable location. Style, yes—but for Kafka, not *Gypsy.*

No walls ruptured the rhythm of the show. Intended to speed the pace by cutting the time for scene changes—which it did—it unfortunately also slowed the pace markedly during the scenes themselves. When there are walls, a character can enter and exit in almost no time because he comes on stage unseen behind a wall and merely has to open a door and appear. When there are no walls, he has to come on stage in full view of the audience and decide how to get to that door at the right moment. He can't race to it without attracting unwanted audience attention, but if he walks slowly, pretending to be invisible while knowing he isn't, trying to time it so that he won't have to wait at the door but can open it on cue the split second he gets there, it may take him almost a minute to cross from the wings to the door. In real time, a minute may not be much, but in theatre time, a single minute can seem like five. Not only is the pace slowed, not only are entrances not the surprise desired, but the audience's attention is split between watching the characters on stage and watching the actor sneaking out of the wings trying to pretend he isn't.

All this prompted more notes from me which Sam tried to deal with. A backdrop with the word "hotel" in huge letters was added to the arrangement of furniture meant to be the hotel rooms. Rose has rented a room for herself and her two daughters but crammed it with the four boys in the act. Along comes a suspicious hotel manager and she has a problem: how to hide the boys from the hotel manager in a set without walls for them to hide behind. While the new backdrop identified the place, it didn't have walls. Rose's problem was still how to hide the boys in a set without walls for them to hide behind. When I directed *Gypsy* four years later at City Center in New York, the production had no walls because we had almost no money. How did I solve the problem of hiding the boys? I cut the suspicious hotel manager: nobody had to hide. Who says the author shouldn't direct?

In truth, I had long wanted to make that cut. The whole section with its farcical running in and out of slamming doors was part of what is called a block-comedy scene. It had nothing to do with the story, but in 1959, when the show was first done, such a scene was a convention of the musical. Even in 1973 in London— particularly in London—it didn't matter that the slamming doors held up the story. The English are brought up on that kind of farce. That was the first time I directed the show, however, and I wanted to kill the author. The scene was a bitch to stage, but it was also a bad detour on the new road I was trying to take the show because of Angela Lansbury, who was *acting* Rose. By 1989, I wanted to get rid of the scene, but with Tyne Daly, who could make sense of almost anything, it was getting big laughs and I didn't have the guts. When I did in 2007, it was because Tom Hatcher had died. His opinion was always my guide; I knew he would have applauded the cut, so with no hesitation and much love, I finally made it. The hotel room played faster, just as funny and so much better for the play, because the story continued to be told.

What that HOTEL backdrop did was exemplify my inability to play the role Scott Rudin had cast me in. I couldn't transfuse the musical sensibility lacked by the director and his designer into their bone marrow. After a while, page after page of notes, particularly the same notes by the author, understandably become an irritant to the director. The author doesn't want to give up on a show he knows and loves. All the same, he has to face that he can't direct by proxy any more than he can transplant the musical in his bones. In the end, practically and artistically, there can be only one voice to call the shots: the voice of the commander-in-chief. That is the voice of the director.

No Walls was in vogue for revivals of American musicals in New York long before *Gypsy*—mainly in productions by British directors, such as the recent ill-conceived *Fiddler on the Roof.* In that new look at an earthy musical, the shabby shtetl where Jews struggled to survive was a polished hardwood floor and a grove of beautiful birch trees with a full orchestra at one side, ready and waiting to strike up the hits. Why would any Jew want to leave? Perhaps because none of the residents were Jews. Never mind that the musical wasn't in any bones on display in this production; sensitivity to the basic material wasn't, either. Tevye, the heart of *Fiddler,* was played by an excellent character actor, but one not right for this show. He lacked the heart, he wasn't musical, and if he was a Jew, it was successfully hidden.

The No Walls concept is not wrong per se for musicals. *Anyone Can Whistle, Floyd Collins,* and *Spring Awakening,* to name three exceptions, would suffocate within walls. Each is without walls not because of a whim or a concept; the work itself calls for a fluid stage. And that's the point—a point as important for a director as having the musical in his bones, if not more so: *everything stems from the basic material.*

Spring Awakening, first staged Off-Broadway, was an exception in another way: it exploded with the first original musical staging in years—the extraordinary work of Bill T. Jones. Like Balanchine and Robbins, who were brilliant both in ballet and on Broadway, Jones is a choreographer with his own dance company but his bones jump with theatre musicality. Although he was not the director, his musical staging enhanced the play immeasurably.

Typical was his use of the microphone that has become deliberately visible in today's musicals because of the hip-hopalong desire to attract a young audience with elements familiar from rock concerts. The "spring awakening" is the awakening of sexuality in teenagers. The shape and size of the mics used by Jones, the way the boys pulled them out of their clothing and held them, didn't leave the audience debating whether "microphone" was a synonym for "phallus." It undoubtedly awakened more sexual fantasies than the real display of phalluses I saw decades ago in a Peter Brook production of Seneca's *Oedipus* at the Old Vic in London, starring John Gielgud and Irene Worth, with the chorus, half-nude, chained to balcony pillars so they could hang without falling off. At the end, everyone sang "Yes, We Have No Bananas" as a six-foot phallus, then an eight-, then a ten- were carried on stage and finally topped by a gilded twenty-footer wheeled down the center aisle. It may have been Seneca and the Old Vic, but it drew a young audience.

I suppose "Yes, We Have No Bananas" could be sung to *Spring Awakening*'s phallic microphones, but will Bill T. Jones and Michael Mayer, the musical's director, still be flourishing four decades from now, as Peter Brook still is, forty years after *Oedipus?* If so, will they be seeking new ways of doing musicals as Brook still seeks new ways of doing plays, or will they still be doing rock? Will I still be doing *Gypsy? Somebody* will be doing *Gypsy.*

Understandably, no director wants to mount a replica of the original production of a musical. But this is often carried to the extreme of refusing to duplicate memorable moments from the original *because* they were memorable, and because the director is too anxious for the production to be hailed as his, with his name in the ad quotes. Actually, it isn't possible to replicate an original, but even if it were, the goal of a revival is to add a fresh take on the material while not losing what made the original worth reviving—

a difficult balancing act. The key is to look at the material with fresh eyes rather than merely with the desire to do something different. Or the desire to sing, like Rose, "For me! For me! For me!"

With *Gypsy*, there's no reason for that problem. Every production is ipso facto going to be different from every other because a different actress is going to be playing Rose, and the production takes its character from her. Visualize Ethel Merman, Angela Lansbury, Tyne Daly, Bernadette Peters, or Patti LuPone as Rose and you know you will see five very different *Gypsy*s. If the director accepts that and molds his show accordingly, his goal is easier, although God knows the execution isn't. If he ignores the essence of his star and insists on fighting both her and the very strong material to impose his "concept," he should not complain if he fails—which he will.

Sam Mendes, like other directors who came to musicals after a reputation made directing plays, came eagerly and stayed. There is almost no one in the theatre in any capacity who doesn't come to the musical sooner or later, perhaps because nothing epitomizes theatre more. Not incidentally, there's also more money to be made. All come eagerly, but few stay or are asked to stay. Playwrights are the least eager, because the book writer's job is the most thankless and garners the least recognition. Yet even Edward Albee succumbed to the lure. At David Merrick's behest, he replaced Abe Burrows as writer and director on the musical version of Truman Capote's *Breakfast at Tiffany's*. That highly anticipated show was a fiasco in tryouts before Edward took over, but after he did, it didn't even open. He did achieve a certain amount of musical-theatre fame, however, with one line he wrote for Mary Tyler Moore as Holly Golightly. To a prison matron, America's then-sweetheart said: "Get your hands off me, you big dyke!" The musical was not in Edward's bones. What *was* in his bones, he attempted to put into the show, but his Holly Golightly and his concept of the world around her was so alien to Capote's that the musical was neither one man's vision nor the other's, and had to fail. Similarly, Sam Mendes's cynical concept of Rose—a character who is forever on a joyous rampage of crazed optimism—and his bleak concept of the Depression world around her had to result in a production so at odds with itself that it, too, had to fail.

If a director comes to musical theatre without the musical in his bones, he can be a liability; if he also insists on his misconception of strongly written material, he will be a fatality. That director would be better off trying to revive a musical that is so weakly written, it might well benefit from a radically new concept. If it succeeds, the director will get accolades. Of course, the acclaim will delude him, but that's not unusual in the theatre—or any-where else. But will it succeed if that director doesn't have the musical in his bones? In a little theatre of his own, perhaps, but not in the arena.

TWO

Guiding Stars

PEOPLE WHO WEREN'T EVEN ALIVE when she was performing know Ethel Merman had the musical in her bones. As did people who never saw her. Seeing her isn't necessary. Hearing that voice does it, and they've heard it in a recording or on a television clip, the unmistakable voice with impeccable diction. No wonder she was the First Madam of Musical Comedy. Could she act? The question was never asked. Even when musical comedy was overtaken by musical theatre, the question wasn't asked. With *Annie Get Your Gun*'s glorious cornucopia of a score, who needed to act? It wasn't asked of her for the less glorious *Call Me Madam* or the inglorious *Happy Hunting*, either. They were musical comedies: nobody was asked to act. When musical theatre arrived for her via *Gypsy*, the question was asked: could the Merm act?

More often than not, the director of a musical theatre piece finds himself searching for exploitable qualities in his stars, actual or so billed, sometimes because of limited acting ability, sometimes because of thinly written roles. Given a pliant actor and a creative director, the resulting illusion fools most of the people most of the time.

Merman was a Roman-candle star who knew how to strut on stage and perform, but not how to act. For *Gypsy*, she needed tutelage—not an unusual task for the director of a musical, but one some directors disdain and some simply don't know how to perform. If it's a star who needs help, that entails standing up to the billing, but most directors have difficulty just getting off their knees. The director in this case shared a history with the star. They knew each other's laundry and they liked each other. He was not very articulate, but he spoke her language. Jerome Robbins was, in fact, the ideal director for Ethel Merman.

His basic problem had nothing to do with his star but was essentially, and remained essentially, his basic problem with the show: his concept didn't come from the material—a common problem for the director who wants the show to be His Show with a box around it. Jerry conceived of *Gypsy* as "a panorama of vaude-ville and burlesque." A panorama is a background; it doesn't focus the show because it doesn't have any relation to the first question the director must ask and answer about any show he is to direct: what is it about? *Gypsy* can be directed to be about various things: parents who try to live their children's lives, children who become their parents, or—what I intended—the need for recognition. Obvious in Rose, the need is common to every character in the play; for the title character, the need for recognition is from her mother—a need for love. That was the point of identification for me as author. Back in 1959 Tom Hatcher and I had been together for five years; my life had been transformed, and it remained so for forty-seven more until death did us part.

Choosing what a show is about is not a textbook choice. Beginning with casting, it influences everything: what the director tells his actors, how he stages them, and where he puts the emphasis in each scene and song.

When Stephen Sondheim, Jule Styne, and I started writing *Gypsy*, Jerry was casting and rehearsing the London company of *West Side Story*. It took us only a little more than three months to finish. By that time, he was trying out *West Side* in Manchester, England, and our show wasn't a panorama of anything. It was the portrait of a woman who has been called the Lear of musical theatre.

For a long time, not only in rehearsal but even out of town in Philadelphia, Jerry refused to accept this. He hired a company for his panorama: vaudevillians and burlesquers—acrobats, jugglers, comics, strippers, showgirls, and dancers. He decided we needed a Minsky Christmas show: a full-length, prototypical burlesque sketch culminating in a big Santa production number. I demurred, arguing that any time neither Rose nor Louise was on stage, we would lose the audience, because we would lose the story. Jerry insisted. I wrote him his burlesque show. It was funny, but so filthy it would be dirty even today in New York. It died in Philadelphia, along with everything else in the show except the kiddie numbers. The Liberty Belles did not want to see their Merm be unpleasant to children—certainly not children presumably hers. Ethel Merman as a mother was itself stretching suspension of disbelief.

The failure of the burlesque sequence sent Jerry elsewhere to demonstrate what Jerome Robbins did for musicals. He tried to cut Louise singing "Little Lamb" to make room for a big dance number in the hotel corridor utilizing all the unnecessary people he had hired. The acrobats tumbled, the jugglers juggled, and the showgirls showed amidst dancers dancing relentlessly. The number had nothing to do with the characters or the story; it was meaningless. Surprising, that, because the first question Jerome Robbins always asked about any dance in a show was "Why are they dancing?" In the hotel, the guests were dancing because Jerome Robbins wanted a big dance number in a show that didn't call for dancing. It lasted one performance.

If *Gypsy*'s director had been a man whose concern was for the show rather than for his position, the choreographer wouldn't have been permitted even to put that dance into rehearsal. It brought the story to a dead stop and eliminated the song that established Louise, who is the heroine. But Jerry was director as well as choreographer, and he was more secure as the latter. Understandably: it was through dance that he best expressed his creativity. Directing, however, gave him complete control.

Words are a director's medium—to communicate with actors, to explicate the text, to uncover the subtext. Unfortunately, Jerry Robbins wasn't comfortable with words. If he sometimes lashed out at actors, it was in frustration because he couldn't find the right words to explain what he wanted. With dancers, language was physical: he could demonstrate with movement; words were footnotes. With dancers, he could command and demand and still receive adulation; with actors, he received stony stares.

When the hotel dance went, Jerry's interest in the show visibly diminished. He felt there was no opportunity to do what he did best. The strip didn't really work; he knew that and had intended to complete it before we left Philadelphia, but he never did, because he had lost interest in Sandra Church, the actress he had chosen to play Louise. She couldn't have been bettered in the first act, but she was lost in the second when Louise becomes Gypsy Rose Lee. She shrank from standing up to Merman in the pivotal scene where Gypsy confronts Rose and levels her. This was an Actors Studio actress who laughingly introduced her own mother as "Rose." Her inability to use that annoyed Jerry; his inability to help her use it annoyed him even more. He gave up on the strip.

Gypsy Rose Lee's success had come from what she said while stripping, not from what she did. I had written remarks for Sandra as Gypsy, but Jerry wouldn't allow her to try using them; she wasn't capable, he said. His interest in her was gone; so was his interest in a musical number he had counted on to show what he could do. He had already created one of the most memorable numbers in musical theatre—"All I Need Is the Girl," which moves and thrills the audience every time. But for Jerry in Philadelphia, disconnected from the show he was directing, unhappy with his lack of opportunity as a choreographer, all he saw was a small number he had knocked off for two characters, one of whom not only didn't dance but, as the number was worked out, was played by me, to whom he had begun to refer to *Gypsy* as "your show."

Theatre egos automatically trigger derision, but a strong ego sometimes is precisely what wins the derby. Ethel was Jerry's choice; he was determined she would be a winner. What he didn't know about acting, he knew about Ethel. He could not have functioned better as a director in the place most vital to the success of the show: Ethel Merman's performance.

It came down to "Rose's Turn." The emotions behind "Everything's Coming Up Roses" she dealt with vocally: that voice was a trumpet call to Armageddon. The scenes were also taken care of vocally. I wrote endless stage directions: "picking up speed . . . getting louder, faster, exploding . . . a pause . . . slower now, quieter, softer." They were all over the script, plus a few "happily"s, "angrily"s, "savagely"s, but tempo and volume worked best. If she was questioned why she was doing what she was doing, she held up the script and, like Adelaide lamenting in *Guys and Dolls,* pointed and said: "It says here, 'faster, louder.' "

Jerry used his version of that technique for directing her in "Rose's Turn." This was unknown territory for her: a complex, coarsely funny, then wrenching dramatic aria, it was set to musical patterns unfamiliar to her. The tricky rhythms were a challenge she could be drilled to meet, but the emotional demands were unchartered waters she would have drowned in had Jerry not been there. He five-six-seven-eighted every moment for her as he would for a dancer, demonstrating as he went: sashaying and bumping, pacing and prowling side by side with her as she mimicked him mimicking her. They didn't probe for subtleties or subtext. He trusted the Sondheim words would speak for themselves if she spat them out with that Merman diction. He was detailed, he was painstaking— and it worked. When she hit that last "For me!" it was Ethel Merman triumphant. She knew all about a show being for her.

Ethel continued to perform precisely as she had opening night. The notes were the same, the voice was the same, all looked and sounded the same; but as the run went on, there was an emptiness, because there was nothing underneath. Jerry had taken her by the hand and led her where she was to go, but *how* she got there and *why* she was there, she didn't know. He wasn't the kind of director who could have told her, but I'm not sure any director could have—certainly no director she would have accepted. She once said: "Buddy DeSylva said watching Ethel Merman is like watching a movie. I never change." It didn't occur to her that someone else might not consider that a compliment. It was true, though: her performance didn't change, not a beat. Not even with Jack Klugman, her leading man, trying hard to keep her fresh and alive. He guided, he cajoled; she revered him, she respected him, but eventually she wore him out. He was, for him, walking through the show right beside her. Still, Ethel Merman's rote was more exciting than almost anyone else's freshness, because there was always that voice. Moreover, her performance had become legendary, and people saw what they had been told they would see. They still see it today, even though they never saw it.

A week after it opened, Merman's *Gypsy* made a dream come true that I'd had since I was a kid. I would arrive at a flashing theatre in my limousine driven by my uniformed chauffeur, walk down the aisle with my lover while the orchestra played the overture to the newest musical hit in town. Well, it was a rented car, but I walked down the aisle with Tom Hatcher, who was far better than the lover I had dreamed, while the orchestra played an overture far better than the overture I had dreamed, to the newest musical hit in town, which I had written but which I hadn't even dreamed. Dreams rarely come true, less rarely are bettered. Small wonder I kept remembering this one—until the other day, when I cut off the memory.

Back in 1959, walking down the theatre aisle with Tom and me was a lovely girl named Kathleen Maguire. She and Tom had met and become close friends in summer stock in Elitch Gardens in Colorado three years earlier. Elitch Gardens with summer stock is long gone, not missed because not remembered, though it very much should be. Kathleen went on to play the lead in an Off-Broadway revival of my play *The Time of the Cuckoo,* which Shirley Booth had starred in on Broadway. Kathleen was better for the play but not for the box office. There, the memory held beautifully. When Tom died of lung cancer, what I had blocked from that memory ten years earlier came unblocked: Kathleen had died of breast cancer.

Even the happiest of memories can be vulnerable. There are others, from other *Gypsys*—more thrilling, more exciting, more lasting, I suspect. But that was my only memory of a dream come true.

Merman's "Rose's Turn" effected two unanticipated changes in *Gypsy,* each calling on a different function of the director. The first began with a mild brouhaha early in the Philadelphia tryout.

Too often the creators of a show think they've made a great point clearly and are puzzled that the audience doesn't get it. We were all so sure, so proud that Rose's admission she had done everything for herself and not for her daughters was not made as it customarily is in musicals—by being spoken in a scene. This being new Musical Theatre, it was sung in "Rose's Turn." But the audience didn't hear it. They wanted Rose to admit she had done it all for herself, and we were certain she did in the number, but the Philadelphia audience didn't agree. In Philadelphia, they were dissatisfied, even with their Ethel.

Time goes fast out of town with a show, even faster when there's an important problem to solve and the only way to solve it is a way you don't want to go: Rose had to admit she did it for herself in dialogue. Reluctantly, a few clarifying lines were added to the brief scene that followed "Rose's Turn," and everyone was happy.

Except Merman. She refused to say the new lines. No Rose she played was going to say she did it all for herself. Steve argued that she had said it in the lyric, why wouldn't she say it in dialogue? "I don't say it in the lyric," she snapped at the lyricist. "I say 'Starting *now,* it's gonna be my turn.' "

Ethel Merman may not have been the swiftest, but she knew what she sang better than the man who wrote the words. She knew better than all of us. We were hearing what we wanted to hear, but it wasn't there.

That was the first and only time Merman refused to do what she was asked. Nor could she be budged. She sat in her dressing room, arms folded, lips tight, waiting for us to admit she was right. She was right about what she sang, but she wasn't right about what was needed for the show and the audience. We all tried to convince her, but it came down, inevitably, to that awkward moment when nobody wants to be the director, including the director. The star has dug in her heels, she has to be moved off the dime. Push has to come to shove, and it's the director who has to do the pushing and shoving. Well, after all, he *is* the director, ha ha ha; he's in charge, it's his show. Otherwise, it's the star's show, and then everyone can go home.

We left Jerry alone with Merman.

The new dialogue went into the show. What he said to her, neither of them ever told.

There is scarcely a show with a star where the moment that defines whose show it is, star's or director's, doesn't arrive, usually in the star's dressing room. When I directed *Anyone Can Whistle,* which Steve and I had written with no regard for conventions, the defining moment came in Lee Remick's dressing room just two days before the New York opening.

One minute after her first entrance in the show, Lee, to a racing musical accompaniment, tore into an extremely long speech so deftly and with such amazing speed that she brought down the house and got an ovation. She was home but not free, for at the end of the scene, she sang her first song, "There Won't Be Trumpets." "Trumpets" is first-class Sondheim, but it's not an easy song and it's rangy. Lee couldn't really sing it. Not only did she not have the musical in her bones, she didn't have much in her modest voice. The number died, hurting her and hurting the show. It was her only song in the first act (of three), but it had to go.

My first hurdle was Steve. He had fantasies about Lee at that time, but he didn't deceive himself about the number. He asked I leave him out of any confrontation with Lee—which I did and as director should have. As Rose says: "You gotta take the rough with the smooth." Nobody more so than the director.

My relationship with Lee had been set the first day of rehearsal. After the reading of the play, I took her to lunch, she being Star One of three (the other two were Angela Lansbury and Harry Guardino). Not your usual movie star, she was bright, genuinely nice and unthreatening. Or so I thought—until even before we had ordered a drink of anything, she said without even a glaze of sweetness, "If Angela Lansbury walks off with the reviews in Philadelphia, I walk."

Philadelphia was where we were having our paltry ten-day try-out. At the first preview, the ladies' room caught on fire, filling the theatre with smoke and panicking the audience; at the third preview, a dancer overran the stage and fell into the pit, smashing a saxophone and sending the musician who played it to the hospital, where he died of a heart attack; and the day of the second preview, Henry Lascoe, the veteran actor who played opposite Angela Lansbury, dropped dead in the wings. A director never knows where help will come from or in what form, but he had better be ready, even for an assist from death.

Unbeknownst to me, Henry had been sabotaging me with Angie. Her role was the commanding mayoress of the town, he was her fawning comptroller; she had the laughs, he had the feed lines. Henry convinced Angie that playing as aggressively as I directed her made her a mean bitch the audience disliked, and so it didn't laugh. The Achilles' heel of most actors—of most people—is the desire to be liked. In the movies, Angela Lansbury had made a career by being a dazzling villainess. Her reviews were always better than good (she was magnificent in *The Manchurian Candidate*), and she was liked by the audience as well. But believing Henry, she played passively. He got the laughs she didn't get, and the audience liked him, not her. Where was I, the director? Stupidly worried that because of lack of experience, certainly in musicals, Angela wasn't able to do on stage what she did so wonderfully, wickedly on screen. Henry rescued both of us by dropping dead. She was forced to drive her scenes and play the character. The laughs came; she heard them; she began having a good time; she gave the audience a great time—and the play got a lot better.

Moral: believe in the actors you cast. If they're not being as good as you thought they'd be, assume it's your fault and find the way to get to them and help them fulfill their potential without killing off the obstructive actor playing opposite them.

Another moral: to retain your own reason in a stressful time—which is what out-of-town with a musical always is—be careful to whom you listen. Kermit Bloomgarden, one of the producers of *Whistle,* a man who regularly produced both Arthur Miller and Lillian Hellman, asked me to heed the advice of a wise man. The man turned out to be his teenage son, on holiday from prep school. Another producer lectured me that the success of a show depended on seemingly small things. Which can be true—but with *Whistle,* the all-crucial small thing was a new dress for Lee Remick, the star. Not too long after her lecture, that producer was hospitalized with Alzheimer's.

Tales like these are routine for directors of musicals, particularly nowadays, when the number of producers is almost as large as the cast, and of that number, perhaps only one actually knows how to produce a musical. The tales are not important in themselves except as theatre anecdotes; what gives them real importance is how congenially the director reacts to the advice, for that affects how forthcoming the money will be to get that new dress, to have more rehearsal time, to market the show. Part of the director's job in this theatre we struggle with today is to direct the producers and the investors along with the actors.

Meanwhile, Lee Remick awaits my answer to her threat to walk.

Her challenge took me completely by surprise, but she *was* a movie star, and no woman becomes a movie star without being a killer. It's cultural, true of any woman in a position of power, political or corporate. Lee, never having been in a musical or having any real stage experience, might have been frightened and in need of reassurance. Whether she was actually frightened didn't matter; I had to treat her as if she was. So I smiled and said, "I'll bet you five dollars"—this was in the sixties—"you'll get the reviews in Philly *and* New York."

The musical was in Angela Lansbury's bones. She was a far superior singer, dancer, performer, and a better actress as well. But the critics, how often are they blinded by a pretty face? Even the gay critics—*especially* the gay critics. Opening night, Lee Remick gave me a mounted five-dollar gold piece.

She wouldn't have if "Trumpets" had remained in the show. When I went into her dressing room to explain why I thought the song should be cut, I told her the truth, at least as I saw it—the only truth anyone can tell, except Fundamentalists, who *know* their truth is The Truth. I think a director must tell his truth. I think everyone in a working situation must, because only truth has a chance of helping. It doesn't have to hurt, as those who don't tell it profess to believe. It's a matter of how you tell it and why you're telling it. If you're really telling it to help, you'll phrase it right.

I didn't tell Lee she wasn't able to sing "Trumpets." I told her the song was wrong for her voice; that that first speech of hers was an aria that got her such an enormous ovation, any song following so soon after was in unwinnable competition; that it left her in an impossible position, one in which, as the heroine of the play, she couldn't afford to be and one in which the play couldn't afford to have her. Left unsaid was that "Trumpets" was her only song in the first act, while Angie had—how many songs?—one more than were originally in the score.

A director has to be a seducer. Before rehearsals of *Whistle* began, Angie sent me a letter from Hollywood withdrawing from the show because her house was in danger of mud-sliding off a cliff, because her children needed her home, because she wanted out. Fear, I decided, rightly or wrongly. I wrote her a letter reminding her that she had made a commitment, that commitments must be honored, that she was an honorable woman, and so forth, but not too much and so on. I meant all of it, but I do good letters, and as this one went on, it became a seducer's letter. And it worked. (Several years later, the situation was repeated with a play of mine she asked to be in and then pulled out of; that time, the seduction didn't seduce. Consistency *is* a hobgoblin.)

She came to New York; we met at Steve's house to discuss the show. Quite quickly the actress who was not appreciated at MGM and had to battle for roles worthy of her displayed what she had learned from the battles. As calm as Lee would be later at that lunch—where do movie actresses learn the code of behavior?—she stated she wanted another song to show another side of the mayoress. Steve and I were so happy to have her back in the show, we would have agreed to a hymn. Of course, it was he who had to do the work, and he did. She got her song: "A Parade in Town." It's one of the best in the show.

Lee knew none of this, fortunately. It would have intensified the already intense tension in her dressing room that day when I told her I wanted to cut "Trumpets." As it was, she sat very still, her face the face from our first lunch. I shut up and waited—a long, silent wait. Then: "I'd like to be alone," she said, and I left.

After an interval, a flurry of mink coats and blue suits from William Morris arrived and marched into her dressing room. Another wait; then a mink emerged.

"The song's out," she said. "Don't mention it. Don't even talk to her for the rest of the day." Then a smile: "She'll be fine."

A good agent. Her name was Phyllis Rabb. No relation to Ellis Rabb, the most imaginative and underappreciated director in the American theatre. If PBS reruns its filmed version of Ellis's production of *The Royal Family* (it's available on DVD), read the play and then watch what a magical director can do with it. Nothing seemed contrived, because everything came from the heart. What a pleasure. What a lesson.

With Tyne Daly in the 1989 revival of *Gypsy,* the defining moment between star and director happened, not in her dressing room, but in the rehearsal room. From the first day of rehearsal, it was apparent she and I were headed for that Showdown at the OK Corral.

I liked her from our first meeting, which was at her audition on the stage of the Imperial Theatre. She had an irresistible smile, a lust for life in the theatre—and great legs. I was surprised how well she sang; the timbre of her voice was oddly similar to Ethel's. This Rose could be sexual, a motor I could use to drive the whole production. From what I had seen of her work, I assumed she was a good actress—perhaps a questionable assumption, since I'd only seen her on TV. She'd begun in the theatre, though, and came from a theatrical family. As it turned out, my assumption was justified: she was a very good actress—a stubborn one, but a damn good one.

She arrived for rehearsal with her beamish smile and armed: she called me "Mr. Laurents." While she didn't overtly question any direction I gave her, there was always the slightly raised eyebrow, the polite question, the little grin that came and went like a sudden threatening cloud on the beach. Unexpressed challenge was always polluting the air, filling the rehearsal hall; the whole company was waiting for the gas to catch fire and explode. Which it did, when we came to the last scene of the first act, where Rose reads June's letter of defection.

Every actress who plays Rose approaches that moment as though she's crawled across the Sahara and seen water at last. She wants to cry and blubber her way into the lead-in to "Everything's Coming Up Roses," even though Rose explicitly says, quote unquote, "This time I'm not crying." Actresses, however, point to the text when it suits them; when it doesn't, they discover subtext.

I had told Tyne Rose is totally without self-pity: she never cries, not a tear, until the final scene of the play, where, in dialogue added pace Ethel Merman, Rose realizes she has never given her daughter the love she wanted. Then Niagara, Victoria Falls—go for all of it. Holding back on tears is unnatural for actresses. Wait two and a half hours before being allowed to go mad with water-works? Very hard, and Tyne wasn't about to wait. She started to cry at the first rehearsal with the first words of the letter speech. The moment had arrived and we both knew it. So did everybody else in the room.

"I told you Rose doesn't cry" was all I said, but it was a fire alarm. Actors, pianists, stage managers, assistant stage managers, all went hurtling for the exit. In thirty seconds, only Tyne and I were left, mano a mano. In retrospect, it seems funny; at the time, it was scary, because it was the moment of Hemingway truth in the bullring for the director and the star. The director loses, he loses control of the show.

A director often has to be a psychologist, or lucky; I was both. I intuited Tyne was challenging me because she *wanted* me to be strong. This was her first musical; it was Broadway bound; she needed a strong director she could depend on to get her there—and more, *belong* there. That meant she would willingly, even happily, go as far as I wanted her to.

It took time. Rose is a rewarding experience, but it takes a good deal of work before her skin fits. Luckily, we had a substantial period on the road. The necessity for that cushion is too often overlooked by directors because they're overconfident. Also, they don't want to trek to Dallas and St. Paul and all the oversized barns in between. By the time we came into New York, Tyne had gone even farther than I asked. Rose was hers, she was *her* Rose—savage, sexy, funny, common as dirt, and absolutely wonderful. And there was a bonus: we had become good friends.

The other big change to *Gypsy* occasioned by "Rose's Turn" began with a piece of advice given by Oscar Hammerstein during the Philadelphia tryout and unfortunately taken. It took fourteen years to rectify the damage.

Hammerstein was in Philadelphia for Steve Sondheim, who made anything but a secret of his gratitude to the mentor who guided his career. But it wasn't Steve Oscar was concerned about when he saw the show in Philadelphia; it was Ethel's bow.

Gypsy is so designed that Rose is on stage alone after a number ends only once in the entire evening. Thus there is only one place for the star to receive her applause and bow in direct response to her audience—at the end of "Rose's Turn." As written, however, just as Rose finishes and starts to bow, Louise comes on applauding, thus killing the audience's hand before it can start and getting the final scene under way. This was exactly what we all wanted. Oscar, however, felt Ethel Merman wasn't getting the applause the audience had been waiting all night to give her; and because they had been waiting in vain, they were frustrated and didn't listen to the last scene.

No matter how grandiose theatre people appear to be or perhaps even are, out-of-town can make the most hubristic unsure of anything. Philadelphia had made us unsure of everything. Even that now legendary overture: at one point new orchestrators kept arriving like immigrants. In addition, this estimation that our failure to give Ethel her due destroyed the impact of the last scene was coming from Oscar Hammerstein, aka God. His advice was heeded: at the end of "Rose's Turn," Rose left the stage while Ethel Merman took her bow. Bows. Endless. She brought the house down and the show went out the window. No one listened to the last scene; it was even suggested it be cut. Ethel was happy, the audience was happy, and if I wasn't, how could I complain? After all, *Gypsy* was a musical and Oscar Hammerstein *was* God.

Fourteen years later, I figured out how we could have our cake and eat it.

Ethel had refused to do *Gypsy* in London. The consensus at the time was that without her, there was no show. By 1973, the show had begun to acquire a reputation; London was eager to see it. Angela Lansbury, who had been living in Ireland helping her children grow up, came over to London to play Rose with me directing. Just the knowledge that an *actress* was going to be at the core of this *Gypsy* made it a very different *Gypsy* in the preproduction in my mind. If she hadn't been Rose, I doubt I would have found how to keep those bows to the audience at the end of "Rose's Turn" and justify them. What was needed wasn't just a musical star but a superb actress and a courageous one: Angela Lansbury.

The solution didn't come from examining the five-six-seven-eight of the "Rose's Turn" choreography or the lyric or even the subtext; it came from going back to why the number was in the show and where it was taking place. Directors of musicals don't do that often enough, not even when they're trying to figure out why a number doesn't work. They'll examine the number, what came before it, the way it's being performed, even *where* it is in the show, but not *why* it's in the show. It's the *why* that will reveal *what* the number is, or isn't but should be.

When I began to write *Gypsy*, I began at the end. The story of Gypsy Rose Lee obviously had to climax with the striptease that gave Louise her name. But even though the show was called *Gypsy*—contractually, it had to be—it was about Rose. Louise's strip couldn't be the eleven o'clock number; Rose had to have that.

Louise would have to settle for the ten-forty-five. The catch was that whatever number Rose did, it had to top the strip, which was more than just a striptease. It was the transformation of a scared, self-esteemless, awkward girl into a confident, sexy, sophisticated young woman—and one who is almost nude to boot. How does a middle-aged woman, star or no, top that?

The answer surprised me, it came so quickly. Louise's strip is topped by another strip, this one by a desperate, crazed middle-aged woman who doesn't actually strip because it's all taking place in the only place she *could* strip: in her recognition-hungry head. It's Rose's turn in the limelight, and high time, too. In her head, she is the greatest striptease queen in the world; in her head, she can bring down the house; in her head, she is the star of stars and can take all those bows. Challenge: how to show they are in her head?

The stage is ablaze with ROSE in huge lights. There's a huge spotlight on Rose as she bows to thunderous applause, even cheers. . . . And bows again. The spot goes with her as she moves to one side and bows again. Then the ROSE lights begin to drop out. She bows again. Now the ROSE lights are gone and the stage light is diminishing. Still, she bows again. Only her spot is left now; the applause is dying out. Her spot is reduced to a dim glow. A work light comes on; the applause peters out, then ends—but not for Rose: she still hears it. She takes a slow, deep, regal bow to deathly silence—and at that moment the audience gets it: there never was any applause for Rose; it was all in her head.

When I explained this to Angie, she thought for a moment and then said: "If it doesn't work, I'll look as though I'm milking the bow."

"It'll work, because you're good."

She gave me a very Angie skeptical look and laughed. "Well, let's give it a try."

We rehearsed with nobody around—no choreographer, no

dance captain, just the two of us and the rehearsal pianist. She had a beautifully cut red dress for the number, but for the preceding scene in Gypsy's dressing room, she herself had bought a ratty gray cardigan in a musty store across the alley from the stage door to wear over the red dress. That sweater was what she used to propel her into the strip: she whipped it off, twirled it around, and flung it into the wings. Everything came easily and naturally to her, except the down-and-dirty vulgarity. That was as natural to Rose as being common, but not to Angie. She had to work hard to get that part of Rose. If Rose had been Cockney, it would have been a piece of cake: look at her Mrs. Lovett in *Sweeney Todd*. But all of it was leading up to the unanswered question: would the audience know everything—every word, every note, every bump, every grind, every bow—was in her head? Would they get that she was bowing to applause that didn't exist, even though they themselves were applauding?

With the second bow, something odd crept into her eyes. You can read Angela Lansbury's eyes from the back of the balcony. They began to dart around. By the time all the ROSE lights were gone and she was taking the last bow in a dim spot, she had made the by-now-unsettled audience aware something was awry; just what, they weren't sure. And then, as she took that last deep bow, she *smiled* to no applause—to a dead silence. She was acknowledging what wasn't there. It was frightening, chilling; it brought an audible gasp from the audience. They got it.

For me as director, it was one of the most satisfying moments I have ever had. That audience went wild. Standing and applauding and cheering Angela Lansbury, yes, but it wasn't Angela Lansbury bowing to them, it was still *Rose*. And she never stopped being Rose. The last scene played as it never had before. Fourteen years, but oh, so worth it.

I don't fault Oscar Hammerstein: that was *his* truth he told. There are times, even in the theatre, when the truth can be an option.

Telling it can be difficult for the director and harsh for the star. That telling depends on who is the director, who is the star, who is the producer, and who cares how much about the show and what is at stake.

During the fourth year of the run of *La Cage aux Folles,* when we were running out of replacements, Allan Carr, the main and original producer, came up with the name of Robert Stack. We had had bigger movie stars who were no longer movie stars—Van Johnson, for one. But Van Johnson had the musical in his bones—he had begun life as a chorus boy on Broadway. His performance was infinitely better than anyone, including Van himself, thought it would or could be. And he was a joy to have in the company. Robert Stack's principal qualification for Allan Carr was that he came from Pasadena. Pasadena makes me think of Barbara Stanwyck and Fred MacMurray planning to commit murder in Billy Wilder's *Double Indemnity.* Or Kim Stanley working as an apprentice in the Pasadena Playhouse. What it made Allan Carr think of was Buckingham Palace: Robert Stack was his Prince of Wales. His musical credential was that he had an aunt who had been an opera singer. Reasoning of that sort was not unusual from Allan when he was coked out of his head, which also was not unusual.

At the time, Robert Stack was more a star than the heavily advertised rap, pop, R&B, TV, MTV, and other DOA meteors who flashed in and out of endlessly long-running musicals—yesterday *Grease,* today *Chicago* (and *Grease* again), tomorrow *Jersey Boys* (wait!)—but he had neither stage experience nor presence. I didn't want him; both authors and all the producers did. Allan really wanted him, and like Lola, whatever Allan wanted, Allan got.

Fritz Holt—one of the producers but also the best production stage manager on Broadway—directed Stack until he was ready to go through the first act. I was called to see what Pasadena had sent to New York. Neither Allan Carr nor any of the other producers nor either of the authors showed up to cheer for their candidate.

Guilt? Fear? Not confidence, not possibly. Only two people were in the auditorium of the Palace Theatre that afternoon: Marvin Krauss, the general manager who had become a producer (ipso facto a Stack advocate) and I. Fritz was fussing backstage like Rose.

To rehearse the role of a piss-elegant middle-aged queen who was the emcee/owner of a transvestite night club on the French Riviera, Stack had chosen to wear jeans, sneakers, and a mono-grammed polo shirt. The outfit was dead right for the way he played the part. When the act was over and Stack was finished, Marvin, who had been shaking with silent laughter much of the time, looked over at me and whispered: "I'm sorry."

Not sorry enough; for he got up and, before he headed up the aisle to freedom from responsibility, muttered, "See if you can get him to quit." If an actor quit, then the producer didn't have to pay him the standard two weeks' salary he would have gotten if he'd been fired.

By the time I made my way up to the stage, there had been an exodus as from Egypt, led, not by Moses, but by the gypsies, the dancers in the show. The gypsies know everything that's going to happen before it actually happens. How they know, nobody knows. But they do, and they did that day at the Palace. Only Robert Stack didn't know. Fritz had vanished. Stack stood there alone, waiting for me to anoint him Star of a Broadway musical.

We sat on the set's furniture, upholstered in mauve silk, facing a papier-mâché giraffe that I had found in Boston and put a dia-mond choker on to make the set look like what people would think was "gay." Stack in his denim jeans sat next to the giraffe, unaware of the diamond choker.

He was very pleasant as we attempted to connect. He had been in a Broadway-bound play with Eileen Heckart. A life raft to seize on: I knew Heckie; she had been wonderful in a play of mine I had also directed. She had been wonderful in the play Stack did with her, too. Where did they do the play? Oh, he and Eileen had begun in a well-known summer theatre in Ogunquit, Maine. And then

Broadway? Well, no . . . it never did get to Broadway; actually, it never got out of Ogunquit. Ah, well, that happens. But he had musical experience? Oh, yes: he had played with the National Symphony Orchestra in Washington, D.C. Played what? The triangle.

I was proud of what had been made of the dicey material that was *La Cage aux Folles.* I loved the company. I was not about to ask them to suffer, gladly or any other way. But I didn't want Robert Stack to suffer from public exposure merely because Allan Carr was a Pasadeniac, and I also didn't want the show stuck for that two weeks' salary.

I ran through all the truisms with the hopeful star. Musicals are very difficult to do if you haven't done one before—on the road, at a dinner theatre, on a cruise ship, someplace, let alone Broadway. Stack nodded. Then there's the difficulty of singing with an orchestra for the first time while on a Broadway stage for the first time. Stack nodded. Whatever I dredged up just brought that pleasant, understanding nod. Finally, a deep, decisive breath and I dove in: he could be doing himself a disservice if he went on. No luck: he nodded; he was prepared for the risk. Of making a fool of himself? Of the newspapers having a field day? None of that mattered, he said. "I can do it if you believe I can do it."

What do you say to that? Truth *and* consequences. No fool he. His performance had been that of a complete amateur, but he wanted the part so badly; his desire was so naked that he had defected from Hollywood. He had exposed himself, he was a person, he wanted the recognition we all want (see *Gypsy*). It was painful to deny him. But then I remembered the triangle in the symphony orchestra. And the opera-singer aunt. And that he was from Pasadena. And what the theatre was about.

"I'm sorry, Bob," I said. "I don't believe you can do it."

"That's that," he said politely, without a trace of resentment, of any feeling at all. We shook hands, he quit that day, and I never saw him again.

I had saved the show his two weeks' salary. When I learned how much, I was in shock: $35,000 a week. In 1986, they were going to pay Robert Stack $35,000 a week! I had saved the show $70,000.

Except that I hadn't. Allan Carr insisted on paying Robert Stack in full. After all, he was from Pasadena.

The absence or presence of movie stars in musicals can be an unexpected trap for an unwary director. The reason for the presence of the movie star is hardly a mystery. No one asks why Antonio Banderas was cast in a revival of *Nine*. As expected, the box-office advance was good. Unexpected were the rave reviews and the wildly enthusiastic audience, both sending the box office skyward. Banderas was completely at home on the stage; his charm was enormous; he was the matinee idol of the twenty-first century; and the company—of women—adored him. If *8½,* on which *Nine* was based, was about a man of genius, and for all that Banderas was, *that* he was not, did it matter? How faithful was the musical to the film, anyway?

The real questions were: What was the purpose of the production? Why was *Nine* revived? Did the director want more than gaudy success? Did he have higher aspirations? Did the authors?

In this theatre, why ask? The show was a success.

The Boy from Oz would not have been the stunning success it was without another movie star, Hugh Jackman. He gave the best performance of any male musical performer in decades as the gay Australian songwriter/singer Peter Allen. (He gave an equivalent performance as the poster-boy American farmhand Curly in *Oklahoma!* in London.) The New York audience went mad for him, as did the box office. Paradoxically, if it hadn't, the producer might have replaced the director, who didn't have the musical in his bones and delivered a very uncertain production which succeeded only because of Hugh Jackman.

His importance to *The Boy from Oz* unfortunately cannot be

overestimated, for a better director might have made it easier even for a star who was obviously enjoying what he did; might even have opened new doors for him, talented as he was, made the work more challenging and exciting, and, best of all, given him a musical play worthy of him rather than a starring vehicle. There is a legitimate need for stars, for reasons poetic and practical, but that need underestimates the importance of the director. There are three, perhaps four, directors who know how to make a musical musical theatre or how to bring out the artist in a star. An illustration is the tale of Patti LuPone and *Gypsy* and the crunching sound of a hat being eaten . . .

THREE

Reviving the Revival

ONCE UPON A TIME, it was said that a certain Playwright swore hell could freeze over before he would allow a certain Star to play the legendary leading role in his legendary musical on a New York stage. Then, lo and behold! Not only did the Star play the role at New York City Center and hell not freeze over, but she was directed by the very same Playwright, in a production that itself was destined to become legendary. This is called Irony, one of the few certainties of life.

In the summer of 2006, Patti LuPone played Rose in a concert version of *Gypsy* at the Ravinia Festival outside Chicago. I was unaware of this until I read the *New York Times* review, in which the critic had reservations about her performance. Every report I heard after that was second- or third-hand. Word came—from where?—that she had a stunning success. More word—from where?—that Margaret Styne, Jule's lovely and perceptive widow, wanted her to come into New York and play Rose; that Stephen Sondheim said her performance had to be seen; that Stephen Sondheim *hadn't* seen her—therefore, did he really say she had to be seen, and who said he did?

Then sharp word—from whom?—that I was the obstacle to LuPone playing Rose in New York. Titillating, but nobody even asked my permission. Also word—from whom?—that it was because she had walked out of a starring role in my play *Jolson*

Sings Again, preventing it from coming to Broadway and angering me so much, I swore no LuPone Rose for a New York stage—ever. While it is true she walked out of an *Off-*Broadway production of *Jolson*—which has never been seen in New York—and also true I was angry at the time, that was many years ago, and I am not an injustice collector. Furthermore, so much of far more importance has happened in my life since then that the incident is as blurred in my memory as my first sexual experience. The metaphor is not accidental; it's a reflection of the importance I place on sex in life. It's in this *Gypsy*—which isn't accidental, either.

Then I was sent YouTube clips of Patti LuPone singing Rose's three big songs at that Ravinia Festival. That was the first time I heard of YouTube, a new fact of life not, I was told, to be taken casually. I assumed the anonymous sender was a demented LuPone fan, furious with me as The Obstacle—until the accompanying message popped up:

"Torture yourself for just two minutes and look at these."

I looked. I saw his (or her) point. She was not a Rose to remember; still, it could not be denied that she could sing the hell out of Rose, not with a Merman trumpet but with a voice as rich, more nuanced, and—for me—potentially more effective dramatically. (I wonder how Merman, with her limited acting ability and musical-comedy face, would be received in *Gypsy* today.)

At that timely point, Scott Rudin called. LuPone had called him because she knew he and I were friends. Scott, who likes playing theatre matchmaker, delayed returning her call until I answered a question. Would I direct her in *Gypsy*?

I had liked her very much the last time I had seen her: in John Doyle's instrumental revival of *Sweeney Todd.* But *Gypsy* takes its tone from Rose. I didn't really know Patti LuPone, so I didn't know what her Rose might be. From the YouTube clips and from interviews she gave on the Internet and TV (risky venues), I wasn't sure she knew, either. If it hadn't been easy for her to call me, I certainly understood; if she had done it because she desperately wanted to play Rose in New York, I also understood. Her call merited a meeting. I don't "do lunch," but dinner could be awkward if we didn't get on, so lunch it was. I invited her to a very Italian restaurant in my neighborhood—she carried on as though she'd been born in Firenze, and the restaurant's waiters carried on as though they thought she'd been.

Lunch lasted three and a half hours. I said almost everything I had to say about some performing ruts she had gotten into. I had done some research and read some interviews she had given about herself—denigrating herself, to my mind—and some she had given about Rose which I thought were way off track. If a director is really interested in who his star is and what she really thinks about the character she would play, he will be wasting time if he doesn't learn as much as he can as early as he can. If he isn't interested, then either he thinks he's the star or he's her stage manager.

Patti's reactions, which included tears, were surprising. Totally uncomplicated was a passionate love of the theatre and a determination to achieve the best she could every second she was on stage. She made an effort to be completely open, and at times she was; at others, she was wary of trusting. The theatre hadn't been particularly kind to her—neither critics, columnists, producers, some of her fellow actors. Nothing had come easily. She agreed that if we were to do *Gypsy*, we would have to start from scratch and take the journey together. And there we left it.

I wasn't sure. Her desire to play Rose had been so paramount, it had gotten in the way of our really connecting. I didn't really know her.

My partner—an inadequate word equaled only by "gay," and is that a coincidence?—my partner, Tom Hatcher, told me to direct *Gypsy* with Patti LuPone. He didn't want the Sam Mendes production to be New York's last memory of *Gypsy*. That wasn't his only motive. He had more on his mind, even more than my doing *Gypsy*.

He knew he was dying of lung cancer, but he didn't want me to know. In retrospect, I'm glad I didn't. He had survived colon cancer. I knew he was having some sort of breathing trouble, but still, that hadn't stopped him from taking our annual three-week ski holiday in Switzerland. I was extremely adept at denial, and since I was unable to imagine a world without him, the possibility that he wouldn't beat this cancer too never occurred to me. Yes, I know; but it didn't.

Looking back, I realize the main reason he wanted me to direct this *Gypsy* was that he knew it would help me if I were busy after he was gone, doing what I liked doing and, in his mind, should be doing. To Tom, I was an unappreciated director who didn't direct as much as I should have. He was certain that with my help, Patti LuPone would finally fulfill her potential and New York would again have a *Gypsy* that *Gypsy* deserved. He urged me to commit—this is hindsight—so he would *know* while he was still here that I would be doing what he believed I should be doing after he was gone. What he asked, I did. But before the production could get under way, cancer won. Fulfilling his wish, my directing *Gypsy* became an act of love.

I didn't know the production was for a limited three-week run at City Center, a Moorish barn just outside the theatre district. It wouldn't have mattered if I had; it didn't matter until I went to work there. I simply wanted to direct *Gypsy* with Patti LuPone, and doing it away from Broadway was a plus to me. Of course I didn't know then what City Center was or how it functioned. If I had, I never would have directed that *Gypsy*—which would have been a whopping mistake. Ignorance can bring unintentional bliss.

City Center was primarily a booking agency for everything from dance companies to tango singers. It hadn't produced a full-scale musical in decades. What it did produce was its very successful Encores! series: revivals of old musical comedies in concert versions—meaning abbreviated texts that actors perform script in hand, wearing suggestions of costumes before suggestions of scenery in front of an on-stage orchestra. Jack Viertel, the artistic director of Encores!—the exclamation point is part of the name— had seen Patti in *Gypsy* at Ravinia and was hell bent on bringing her to City Center to launch its new Summer Stars series. Jack was the de facto producer of *Gypsy*—unacknowledged, because he was employed by, and thus under the jurisdiction of, the Center's Ninth Floor, where its managerial offices emulate Dante's Ninth Circle of Hell. This is best illustrated by an e-mail from the Floor's Führer.

He made it clear that this was a City Center production and would be done in the City Center way. If we pushed back he would "nickel and dime [us] at every turn."

If the Ninth Floor had read the front page, they would have known how important the e-mail is as evidence of stupidity as well as cupidity. To them, *Gypsy* was just another Encores! with a few extra trimmings.

Fortunately, I didn't have to take them on alone; I had what every director must have, even in a situation that isn't ugly: a production stage manager who could fill in any blank I couldn't. Craig Jacobs, the best PSM I know, enabled me to do the production I wanted despite City Center. It was never easy or smooth going, but that didn't matter. I was more excited by the work I was doing than I had been for a long time—maybe ever, because I wasn't seeking anyone's approval.

As it turned out, Tom would have been more than pleased. So I thought when we opened. Over time, I progressed from thinking he *was* pleased to believing he *is* pleased. Yes: is. And that has made life pleasurable again. No one would have smelled incense and heard temple bells or scoffed at that more than I would have back before the moment when all went lopsided and changed so radically. But dealing with death can make a skeptic deal with possibilities that weren't acknowledged, let alone accepted. Dealing with death is dealing with how to go on living—in my case, what had been a wonderful life. The summer of City Center, I got an e-mail from Mike Nichols about *Gypsy* that I wished so much Tom had read; today I believe of course he *has* read it and is infinitely pleased for me that *Gypsy* had made Mike Nichols "realize again and for the first time in a very long time that the theatre is still the best thing we have."

No praise means more than praise from a peer you respect and admire. It came in other e-mails, in notes and phone calls from friends, acquaintances, people who were just familiar names in the theatre, even a bona fide critic, however former: Frank Rich. Long a fervent admirer of *Gypsy*, he saw the production three times during its brief run and sent me an ecstatic e-mail.

What made Mike Nichols and Frank Rich, what made others, what made all of them react so strongly to this *Gypsy*? What made the audience cheer and scream all during the play at every performance? What made closing night the most extraordinary night I've ever seen or heard of in the theatre?

More than 2,500 people, from the celebrities in the orchestra to the audience in the third balcony, stood and applauded and hollered and cheered for almost fifteen minutes. Fresh roses made it difficult to walk on the stage. "None of us had ever experienced anything like that in our careers," said the City Center's stage-management report. "We chose ultimately to leave the curtain out. We brought the houselights up, the audience remained in place, screaming itself hoarse and clapping its hands raw. As the company disappeared into the wings, a brief but undeniably significant chapter in musical theater history came to a close."

"Significant" additionally because this was not the premiere of a new, innovative work that might change the course of musical-theatre history; this was the closing night of the *fourth* New York revival of a show half a century old. Nothing new on paper—but there must have been something new somewhere. Not a new star, because even with bigger and brighter stars, there had not been a response remotely close to this on the closing, or for that matter opening, night of the original or of any of the other revivals.

Why that extraordinary response to this particular production? What process made the production itself extraordinary?

I had directed *Gypsy* twice before, and while each production was inevitably as different as the Rose played by two very different stars, and each was a still remembered success, I had no interest in repeating either Angela's deeply probing yet deftly comedic performance of a Rose in conflict with herself or Tyne's earthy, brassily comic performance of a driven, sexual Rose or a variation of either. Losing Tom had changed my priorities: the theatre didn't matter as it once had. If I was going to participate in life, it could only be in theatre; but without him, it could only be theatre that really excited me—certainly not a revival that was just another revival. Because it was for him, this *Gypsy* had to be a *Gypsy* completely unlike any that had ever been seen, and not only because Patti LuPone being Patti LuPone would be a Rose unlike any other anyway. It would be an Event; Patti would take the town by storm, and the production would wake up the New York theatre as Tom wanted and predicted.

That was the goal: an Event. How I would make this fourth revival of *Gypsy*—I didn't really think "fourth," I wasn't counting—how I would make it an Event, I had an inkling, but not a doubt that I would until City Center's Ninth Floor made execution of that idea, or any idea, unlikely.

Example: their schedule for technical rehearsals was a candidate for senselessness. Of the five days they offered, the first day was without a crew, which made rehearsal pointless; the third day was the Fourth of July, a holiday at the Center, which meant no rehearsal, because no one worked; and the fifth and last day was reserved for a special run-through for their board (of investors), sitting in the mezzanine because photographers would be in the orchestra taking production shots of a production that didn't exist.

The schedule for technical rehearsals should be made by the production stage manager and the director, who have worked with the scenic designer and know all the various artistic needs of the production. They then submit their schedule to the producer(s) and general manager for comment. City Center's Ninth Floor wasn't the first and won't be the last of the current breed of producers to reverse the order. Their concern is money, not quality, and even before that, control. Control of exactly what, they aren't sure, but if they have it, they can decide what is worth being in control of.

Craig Jacobs came up with a workable schedule that was ultimately accepted after a battle that was disgusting even for the Ninth Floor. It had a positive effect, though. It forced me to face that if *Gypsy* was going to be the Event I envisioned, I had to ignore the producers and, with Craig's help, do as I wanted. Actually, what could they do? They were promoting the show, they were selling the show, they *needed* the show.

There's always something that can be done by any side. What they could do, they did. As warned, they nickeled-and-dimed the budget for scenery and costumes. There are two ways to deal with that: quit, or take it as a challenge to let imagination and inventiveness supplant money. A big Broadway musical costs far too much these days, anyway: there's too much reliance on too much scenery and too many unnecessary costumes and too little courage to push the audience to use *its* imagination by directors and creators using theirs—and too much acceptance by producers and general managers that this costs that much. "Why?" you ask. "Because it just does," they answer. Well, examine it; question it; often, it doesn't.

I began with the costumes. To suit the limited budget, my idea was for the show to be the world as seen through Rose's eyes. In the first act, the only costumes that would register would be for Rose and June—Baby and Dainty—and Louise. For the vaudeville acts, the kids, big and little, would be costumed as little as Rose could get away with on her "Eighty-eight bucks." For the character women, a generic dress with an accessory for the occasion—cloche hats for the mothers at *Uncle Jocko's Kiddie Show,* a coolie hat for the Chinese waitress in the resturant, collar and cuffs for Miss Cratchitt in Grantziger's office. Similarly, for the character men: shirts and pants, with a plaid tam for Uncle Jocko, a cap for Georgie, suspenders for Pop in the kitchen, a suit and tie for Weber backstage at the vaudeville house.

As the play and Rose moved along, more costumes would appear. When June left, Louise's costumes would be stepped up to stand up to Rose. In the burlesque house, more characters in more costumes, until by the end of Louise's strip, the company would finally be in full costume for a full production number in a Broadway show.

The costume designer I chose was Martin Pakledinaz. We had met more than twenty years ago when he was assisting Theoni Aldredge on the surpassingly brilliant *Cage aux Folles* costumes. We had been glad to run into each other occasionally over the years, usually through Theoni, but Marty had come into his own with fireworks. Working together can be a strange test: how was he going to react to my strong ideas? He was one of the very few good costume designers around, I wanted him, we *had* to work well together. We did, and better than merely "well." I didn't anticipate how exhilarating it would be.

Presumably the director chooses a design team for its excellence and expects or hopes it will and can follow his lead. Sometimes, as with *Wicked,* where great slabs of scenery have nothing to do with the story, perhaps the director didn't choose the designer—or perhaps he did but the designer went off on his own. How those slabs got on stage and stayed on stage is another question. In a musical where no one is completely in charge, anything can happen, and often does. When the director is in charge (as I was despite the Ninth Floor) and he's chosen a great design team (as I had despite the Ninth Floor), it's exciting to see what the designer does with the concept handed him. Marty Pakledinaz took mine to a place I hadn't imagined by adding a brilliant use of color to tell Rose's story.

In the opening scenes, the center of her world and her dreams is Baby June, too radiant in a Dutch-girl costume of a glaring sky blue. Louise's Dutch-boy costume was a cloudy gray-blue. All the other costumes were almost colorless. Uncle Jocko's tam and knee britches were a washed-out Scotch plaid; the balloon girl's balloons were the blandest balloons ever blown. Only Rose had color—not as bright as June's, but suiting Rose's vulgar taste.

One exception: she wore an old paint-smeared smock when she was working on the vaudeville numbers or Louise's strip. That paid off in the one dress Marty and I disagreed about. She was covered by the smock for "Rose's Turn"; when she came to "Here's Rose!" I wanted her to tear it open and there was Rose in that Red Dress. Marty said every Rose wore that Red Dress. He was right, but it was the color we were building to all night; and the use of that dress illustrated an important cautionary note for the director of a revival: merely because something was done with notable success before, don't throw it out unless you can do better. It's hard to do better than a Red Dress at the climax of *Gypsy*. No color can outdo red. Particularly when you don't see it coming, which, because of the smock, this time you didn't.

Marty held back color in the first act, but in the second he brought it out in an imaginative use few designers are capable of today. At the end of act one, the older Louise wears a shapeless, colorless blouse, as usual; in the first scene of act two, June is gone, Louise still wears a shapeless blouse, but the blouse is now blue, June's color—not June's Easter-egg blue but a blue strong enough to put Rose on guard and pay attention: Louise is now a challenge.

As the play moved into burlesque, there were the strippers. Of course they needed color, but not strong enough to overwhelm the deliberately chosen first moment of pure color: when Louise, for the first time in a dress, looks in a pier glass and says: "Momma, I'm a pretty girl."

Instead of putting Louise in a black evening gown for her first awkward strip, as had been done in the very first *Gypsy*—what stripper in a cheesy burlesque house would wear black?—Marty put her in a soft lavender, a color Tessie Tura would wear, because the dress is one Louise presumably has been making for her. And instead of pouring Louise into a shimmering sequined Vegas gown for the last scene, as every other designer had, Marty slipped her into a draped *gray* silk dress with long sleeves and a high neck. Elegant but too quiet? Not what Gypsy Rose Lee would wear? The dress had a slit up the back bordered with rhinestones that weren't seen until at the end when Gypsy turned and her back was to the audience as she walked out on Rose.

When I asked Marty why he put Louise in that chic gray dress, he quoted Rose's line to Louise: "You look like you should speak French."

A designer motivated by the text! All designers read the script; their designs show if they understand it. If they don't, the director must explain it to them. If the designs still don't show understanding, the director tries again. After that, accept you made the wrong choice and move on. Choosing Marty was hitting a bull's-eye.

Jack Viertel agreed with the Ninth Floor about the placement of the orchestra. The junta was determined it be on stage because it always was on stage for Encores! I was equally determined it not be on stage for *Gypsy,* which they still wouldn't admit wasn't an Encores! production (they never did). For them, the orchestra on stage left less room for scenery, thus making the physical production cheaper and freeing the pit for more top-price seats. For me, the orchestra on stage would expose the actors to playing a play, not a précis, in front of an unwanted audience of musicians on a bandstand as in Encores!

It wasn't too hard to win. It's not difficult to awaken guilt about money in most opponents in the theatre, particularly City Center, where it never slept. "Star" is a synonym for "money" there; *Gypsy* was to be the first production in the new City Center series, Summer Stars. Patti LuPone was a star. Patti didn't want to play intimate scenes in front of an orchestra. They agreed the orchestra would stay in the pit where it belonged.

Except that it didn't.

By the time the company got on the stage for rehearsal, the orchestra was on stage. With my full agreement. What had happened? Money.

Jack Viertel came to me with a proposal: he could get an extra $200,000 out of the Ninth Floor for the physical production if I agreed to have the orchestra on the stage and freed up the space for more high-price seats down front. That $200,000 was the equivalent of an extra $2,000,000 for a comparable production on Broadway. In the theatre, as everywhere, the modus operandi is to accept or reject flat out rather than make an effort to figure how it might be possible to have it both ways. I wanted the money; I did not want the actors to play in front of the orchestra on stage—but that was where the orchestra had to be for me to get the money. There had to be a way for both Jack and me to get what we wanted. I went to Jim Youmans, our scenic designer.

City Center's stage is extremely deep, so deep that I had asked Jim to cut the stage in half with a scrim. Jim smiles more than any other designer I have ever worked with; the smile is both real and a cover for one of the most interesting and endearing people in the theatre. Behind the scrim, he halved the stage with another scrim, the area between the two reserved for Rose's fantasy world. Jim is the most talented designer of minimalist scenery I know; but this wasn't about scenery, it was about space. The question that needed an answer was: if we put the orchestra against the back wall and put a third scrim in front of it, could we have all the musicians on stage without their being seen? Jim measured; we could. Without those little lights on their music stands being seen? A black scrim would hide them, he assured me.

When you get what you want, you want more. I began searching for moments when the orchestra on stage could work to the advantage of the play. Three popped up immediately: during Tulsa's number, during "Rose's Turn," and, most potently, during what is arguably the best overture to a musical. For me, the only possible rival is *Candide,* but after its overture, the music for the play is thwarted.

Gypsy would begin by having rich red curtains part and scrims lift, one by one, to reveal the orchestra, painted with light as only Howell Binkley can. Seeing the dramatically lit orchestra play that overture would silence the chatter that customarily goes on during overtures; instead, the show could start the audience on a high. But then what? The Jocko scene would have to be a letdown unless something unexpected happened before it started. And something did. As the overture came to its end, the scrims that rose to reveal it came down in the same sequence in which they came up, the last being a black scrim that blotted out the orchestra during the closing bars in time to bring down a peeling gilded portal, holes in its rotting frame and rips in its hanging, tattered swags, that said Dead Vaudeville/Dead Dreams. That portal set the tone for the whole show. It startled the audience: this was not going to be the *Gypsy* they expected. But they applauded the overture and cheered—something they had never done before.

The theatre audience has not necessarily been dumbed down by what's presented to them these years. It still has an imagination, and it still can use it, even with revivals. It's hungry to see a new light on an old scene.

Paradoxically, what started this *Gypsy* on the road to that memorable closing night was another of the Ninth Floor's inadequate schedules, this one the heedless lack of rehearsal time.

On West Forty-fifth Street, I would have been given four or five weeks with the full company. On West Fifty-fifth Street, out of the central Broadway district, City Center scheduled two weeks with the full company. I bargained: if I used only the four leading players and one pianist, could I have one more week? Jack agreed and got the Ninth to agree. I took that as an opening: with his help, I managed, player by player, to inch the number up to nine.

We started sitting around a table that first day—Patti LuPone, Boyd Gaines, Laura Benanti, Leigh Ann Larkin, Jim Bracchitta, four other actors, and I. Except for a piano in the corner, it might have been the first rehearsal of a play, not a musical. The picture was familiar. For the last ten years, most of my work in the theatre has begun sitting around a table at the George Street Playhouse across the river in New Brunswick, New Jersey, with its unique artistic director, David Saint. George Street seeks new plays; David, who has directed several of mine, is the best director who ever has. *Venecia,* a new play Tom and I found in Buenos Aires, David produced at George Street. Tom translated; I adapted and directed, with Chita Rivera starring as the old blind madam of a whorehouse with one customer. A lot of rehearsal time was spent sitting around the table even though *Venecia* is fantasy, farce, and even has a musical number. When I revised and directed *Hallelujah, Baby!* that began around a table too. We didn't stay around the table as long as we should have. Well, it *was* a musical. Why, then, did I stay around the table with *Gypsy?*

So much of *Gypsy* is about growing up and older that it needs to be rehearsed in sequence. That was impossible at City Center, because the little kids were absent from rehearsal. It was also impossible to stage more than a piece of a scene, because even though the nine players included character men, there was always one character who wasn't covered. So there we were that first day with nothing we could do but sit around the table: nine players and I like nine actors sitting around a table with a director for a play. *Gypsy* wasn't a play, it was a musical; musicals aren't rehearsed sitting around a table. But it wasn't a musical comedy, it was musical theatre; it might even be a musical play. Couldn't it at least be rehearsed as though it were?

The first thing I said to the nine players was "*Gypsy* is a musical for actors."

In 1959, it hadn't been cast that way; in 1959, acting was hardly a priority in musicals. It's of incalculable help to the director of a revival to look back at the state and customs of the form (in this case, the musical), the theatre in general, even the world at the time of the original production. Then he can begin to understand why certain moments seem foolish today while others weren't given their due back then. *Gypsy* has its share.

In 1959, Ethel Merman was the star; she set the breezy tone. In 1973, in London, Angela Lansbury was the star. A superb actress with a great voice, her Rose gave *Gypsy* a weight and meaning it hadn't displayed before. That it did then was almost entirely due to her Rose. In 1989, that process continued with Tyne Daly, the star making history with her savage Rose, but she was aided immeasurably by the first three-dimensional, moving Herbie, played by Jonathan Hadary, and the first credibly bland Louise to turn into a dazzling Gypsy Rose Lee—Crista Moore. It wasn't until 2006, however, that I cast the entire company—everyone, every small part, even one-line parts—with first-rate actors. Why shouldn't acting be as important a requirement for musical theatre as singing and dancing?

Everyone around that table at City Center was an actor, and every part got bigger because I asked everyone to know who he or she was in the play, why they were in the story, and what they wanted in any scene they were in, even if they didn't have a line. The fuller the character, the bigger the part becomes. When the whole company was around the table, that approach was applied to everyone: Why was someone a Hollywood Blonde or a Farmboy? Why had they joined Rose's traveling circus? Did they want to be in show business, did they want to run away from home?—

what did they want? Even if they didn't have a line, they had to know all that. This wasn't going to be a musical where anyone came on stage without a life.

What I expected from the nine major players by the end of the first week was that each would know who he was, what he wanted, and what he would do to get it. The excitement around the table that first morning was visible—but no one had to be cautioned that *Gypsy* was a show with a Star.

If the star of a play, let alone a musical play and one with a starring role that has been called the musical equivalent of King Lear, if that star isn't with the director all the way in every way, the tension will infect the company and nothing much will ever be accomplished. Play or musical, the performance will waffle and wobble and satisfy no one. The star at this table was Patti LuPone: famously controversial, a powerful actor with a great voice for Rose. Great voices, great anything, can get in the way of a great performance unless the director is in control. Nothing was going to get in the way of this performance: Patti LuPone was indeed a star, but she was an artist first. There's a self-consciousness about calling anyone an artist, but she was and always will be, certainly in the rehearsal hall. Nothing could make her happier than sitting around the table, probing and exploring the text. She gave herself completely to the process with constantly stunning results. The company loved watching her work, loved exploring with her, loved *her*—to a point: they smelled the actress might turn Star on a dime. Rarely in rehearsal, but on stage, in performance, there was the danger that she would become too aware of the audience, wanting to possess it, control it, make it hers—the Star would trump the artist. That was her problem, which made it the director's problem, which made it *my* problem. She trusted me early on and I respected her early on. Nothing was going to separate us, and nothing did. But I was conscious of that Star problem and she wasn't.

Of the six days of rehearsal that first week, five were spent around the table. They were the most important days of the entire rehearsal period. Musicals had never been directed this way— every line examined as one does or should do when rehearsing a play—because no one thought the book of a musical could stand up to such examination. The high regard for the book of *Gypsy* might be used as an excuse for making it an exception to how musicals are rehearsed, but it shouldn't be. Even a musical with a weak book can benefit from sitting around a table and exploring what text there is. All sorts of moments can be found in unexpected places; subtext can be invented where none existed to give characters some depth and color. Look for the *play* that is beneath the *show* and the result will be a richer evening. There isn't a musical that won't benefit from adding acting to performing.

Those days of exploration around the table established for the actors what their goal was and how it was going to be achieved. They got what they had never so early, if ever at all, had before: a solid base from which they could move out and try this or that, knowing there was a secure core of the character underneath. It was still a musical, but they were taking it seriously as *actors* because they were being treated as actors. They thrived on it, so the show thrived on it. The result was a *Gypsy* new to everyone, including me.

I had written the book of *Gypsy*, ostensibly based on Gypsy Rose Lee's memoirs; three-quarters, however, was invention—which was why I called the show a "fable." I had directed it twice before, each time seeing it from a different angle because of a different Rose. Yet, sitting around that table, I kept making discovery after discovery about every character, beginning with Rose and Uncle Jocko in the opening scene. Directing a revival of *Gypsy* became as exciting as directing a new play. I was charged up, as creative as I had ever been. My ninetieth birthday was a month away, but when you are caught up in giving new life to something you love, you are whatever age you were the first time you gave it life.

The opening scene of *Gypsy* was key. Usually it's played with Jocko a comic trying to eke out a laugh until the star playing Rose makes her famous entrance down the aisle and takes over the audience, the stage, and the show. Musical theatre, perhaps, but not a musical play—not even a scene in a musical play, because a scene requires at least two of the people on stage be fleshed-out characters who interact. This time, for the first time, Jocko became a character and Rose became more than a star doing a turn.

All the actors needed was there in the script—if the director looked for it and led them to it. Jocko has been doing his *Kiddie Show* so long that he's sick of it—sick of the mothers, sick of the kiddies, sick of the audience, sick of everything except a sexy girl probably too young for him. Her sister is a contestant, which makes her blatantly a shoo-in. Playing Jocko is tricky, because he must be likeable enough for the audience to enjoy him but not so likeable that the audience will resent Rose for destroying him. Everything serves the story.

Watching from out front, Rose must have seen the favoritism, but gives no sign of it when she climbs on stage. She's seemingly just a mother concerned with her daughter-contestant, Baby June. All friendly charm, Rose prances over to Jocko, smiles down to the drummer, waves to the lighting man—happy with herself, happy with her girls. Then Jocko laughs at her and Rose turns on him like an adder. The scene—it is now a scene—explodes: the play has begun.

Once that process started, *Gypsy* is such a rich field that the actors couldn't wait to dig into all the scenes. The deeper they dug, the still deeper they wanted to dig. When had rehearsals for a musical been exciting merely by exploring the text of a scene? Never; the text of a musical had never really been explored. Now, the company couldn't wait to get back to that table, explore more, go farther or correct and refine. Even during previews, we went back to the table.

But what of what the audience comes for, the musical numbers? *Gypsy* is famous for them but they became a problem I hadn't foreseen because of an incident with Laura Benanti at her audition.

Louise is a very difficult part to cast: she begins as an awkward, vulnerable, not noticeable teenage tomboy and ends up a glamorous, sexual, sophisticated, tough Star. I had seen and been interested by Laura Benanti on stage, but nothing had prepared me for what she did at that audition. Clearly, she had it all and could do it all. My sole concern was whether she would respond to direction from me. I asked her to sing "Little Lamb" again, but with a different approach, one I had been thinking about when I began taking a fresh look at the show:

Louise is really miserable when she sings "Little Lamb." There was the perfunctory verbal acknowledgment of her birthday and a few skimpy presents, but the focus as usual and always was on June and The Act. A line that had always been in the lyric now justified the approach: "Little cat . . . why do you look so blue? . . . Is it your birthday, too?" By the time Laura got to that line, tears were glistening in her eyes; by the time she got to the end of the song, tears were in the eyes of everyone in the room.

That was encouraging, both about Laura and about a fresh approach to the songs. Encouragement, however, can lead to expectations, and expectations are a one-way ticket to disappointment. At the start of rehearsals, Laura Benanti was unsure and not very good, certainly not as good as I was convinced she could be, and wary of me, to boot. I was fertile with explanations, but from Marty Pakledinaz, whose costume fittings can often be confessionals, I learned that Laura's previous show had been a bad experience for her because of the director: an explanation I hadn't thought of, and one that was reassuring—but the next director invariably pays, I was paying, and if it continued, we both would be in trouble. How was I to get her trust? That's a problem every director has with every actor to some extent, and every director has his or her own way of dealing with it, from heart-to-heart talks to ignoring it. My way was to treat Laura Benanti as the actress I believed she was and try to help her as that actress. What was her *acting* problem? Trying to play young rather than what the young Louise was feeling. In a quiet corner of the rehearsal hall during a break, I told her that and just that. No bells rang, no tears came to her eyes; she didn't throw her arms around me; but it was a seminal moment all the same. She relaxed—visibly. Sitting around the table, we started discussing what was going on inside Louise, how overtly she would express it, and when signs of the woman she was going to be would begin to appear. She now came early to rehearsal, she loved rehearsing, and I loved directing her.

The right button is what the director always has to find, the button that will free the actor to give the performance both want. That means the director being ready to take anything and try anything, even if it means making a fool of himself. I had found the right button to press for Laura, but there was one place where the only way to help her was to risk making a fool of myself—so what the hell, I did. To her enjoyment and the enjoyment of the few people allowed in the rehearsal hall, I simulated the strip for her. I may have looked like a fool, but it was obviously fun; fun helps rehearsals.

The transition in that striptease from Louise as a naïve, untalented, awkward young girl into the sexually sophisticated, secure, witty Gypsy Rose Lee is an extremely difficult challenge for any actress. Laura took it in stride. She understood it emotionally, she was confident she could do it. The physical act of stripteasing was another matter, unknown territory. She'd never seen one, and willing as she was to try, she didn't have a clue where to begin. Underneath, she was afraid. She is very beautiful, with a beautiful body, but very far from being an exhibitionist—judging from how she dressed at rehearsal, the opposite.

How she moved had to come from who she was playing. At that early stage, I knew who that was probably better than she did. So with the help of a drummer and Patrick Vaccariello, our musical director, who was in happy sync with anything I wanted to do musically and became enjoyably essential to me as work progressed, but without the help of our ready, able, loveable, and stoical choreographer, Bonnie Walker, I walked a striptease for Laura Benanti. If I could do it, she could do it better: she had more to work with. As we went through each of the four strips that make up the number, she brought two elements that were all Laura Benanti and made the strip strikingly hers. One was an idiosyncratic sense of humor completely unexpected in a woman so beautiful; the other was a stripper's walk that Gypsy Rose Lee would have lusted for. From fearing the strip, she went to loving it and then, actress that she is, to perfecting every detail tirelessly. The curtain I had planned to use to end the number couldn't work with the City Center set—a situation directors have to face constantly. This time it was fortuitous, because a new ending was needed, something as special as Laura. Examining what curtains were available in City Center's archives, I found how to end the number with a use of curtains not seen before. In Rose's biblical mode, seek and ye shall find—so long as ye know what ye're seeking.

The fresh approach to "Little Lamb" that misled me into thinking the music was not going to be a problem helped me be alert to possible problems the music could cause before they happened. At the outset of rehearsal, lyrics were spoken and explored around the table just as the dialogue was. The first book song, "Some People," was a little difficult to bring off as sort of a soliloquy in a musical play; it seemed more the star's opening number. It's difficult for Rose to get into the song vocally: she has to slam in on all cylinders. Helping her get there emotionally would help her get there vocally, but Patti wanted to start easy. She had such a great voice, knew so well how to deliver, I didn't push her. A mistake. The audience screamed and yelled, but it was still a mistake. At least I was aware of it. I was also aware there was nothing I could do about it at that moment, so I moved on to Rose's duets with Herbie—eagerly, and why not? Both have lyrics that are layered and begging to be explored—and who better to explore them with than Patti LuPone and Boyd Gaines, the last of the great leading men because he is also a great character actor. Still, he had a button I needed to push.

I knew what it was before we started rehearsals. Boyd Gaines is reticent by nature. He is afraid of overdoing, of being in the way, even of asserting himself. So is Herbie. When Herbie finally erupts, it should come as a welcome shock. But I wanted signs of it earlier in this Herbie; I didn't want it to come from nowhere. Boyd is such a good actor, he can do that with one word— the word "no," as a matter of actual fact. When he tells Rose in the Chinese restaurant that he is afraid of walking out and she laughs it off with "Only around the block," Boyd's *"No!"* said this man was much more than he seemed. Only one word, but it achieved a big purpose and launched her into "You'll Never Get Away from Me."

Boyd himself has an offbeat sexiness and a sense of humor he can use physically that I wanted him to exploit but which he feared might get in the way. Whose way? Patti's? Patti LuPone loves actors who give her something to play off. Pushing Boyd Gaines to let go was not easy; he is so used to being a gentleman. But what is there to lose by going too far with a good actor? I pushed and pushed so hard it stirred him to let go and let fly. He and Patti had a sexual chemistry; they meshed like the answer to a director's dreams. The result was musical scenes so clearly what they always should have been that I wondered why I hadn't directed them that way before. Certainly they were much richer than they ever had been. I wrote them: didn't I know what I was writing? Does any writer know all he is writing—know what's underneath what he has written? Not if he's any good, is my guess. But he does need actors and a director to give life to what's there, and I had a pair like those they don't make anymore—the Lunts, Gertrude Lawrence and Noël Coward—in this *Gypsy:* Patti LuPone and Boyd Gaines. Rehearsals of their scenes made the days too short.

Their songs, however, were written for characters in a story; their potential was inherent. As scenes, they had an unexpected and unfortunately undesirable effect; they highlighted another unanticipated musical problem: some songs didn't belong in the show now, not the way the show was being played. They were simply musical-comedy numbers, meant only to entertain. They had never been intended to be anything but musical-comedy numbers meant only to entertain. The story didn't need them; there were no layered lyrics—clever lyrics, yes, lightly comic lyrics, yes, but lyrics that simply said what they said, period. No subtext, no text of much consequence at all. What rabbit could be pulled out of what hat to make them fit into a musical play?

No composer and lyricist knew more about writing a theatre song than Jule Styne and Stephen Sondheim; why, then, were those songs written like musical-comedy numbers? Because of *when* they were written—1959, the Golden Age of Musical Theatre. But musical comedy had not been banished. Every show, even the most aspiring and ambitious, paused routinely for songs that were meant to be just entertainments or showstoppers or simply "divertissements," as Lenny Bernstein called *West Side Story*'s "I Feel Pretty" and "Gee, Officer Krupke." (His linguistic virtuosity prompted me to write a stage direction for *West Side:* "Braggadocio and Con Brio cross upstage hand in hand.") The contrast of "If Momma Was Married," for example, with the musical scene "You'll Never Get Away from Me" as Patti and Boyd were playing it, made "Momma" seem even more a number in another show. It was essential that it be pulled into the play, because it came at a turning point in the story. That made it the first real challenge to this *Gypsy* being a musical play.

Less than midway through the first act, there is a scene between June and Louise, two sisters who barely know each other. With no warning or reason but lots of clever rhyme and a bouncy Viennese vamp, the girls launch into "If Momma Was Married." The melody is very pretty, the lyric is cleverly comedic, and combined with terrific close harmony at the end, the song brings down the house. It probably would have worked as it was even in this *Gypsy*. But that scene, brief as it was, was dense, packed with emotion no June until Leigh Ann Larkin had ever shown. Where we were with both sisters in the scene and with what it had become, I didn't want to settle for what "worked."

No rehearsal day is productive if the director hasn't had to choose whether or not to settle for what "works." With "Momma," there was no choice. The sisters themselves and their relationship had become so complex and involving, and far too much subtext had surfaced, to allow them to bounce girlishly into a bright waltz. I knew Patrick could augment musically any new note I came up with, but what I had to come up with was how to get those girls into the bloody song; how to get the song into the scene. It had to be part of the scene, because it came at a point in the act where it would tell the audience either that this was a very different *Gypsy* or that this was a *Gypsy* that didn't know what it was.

The key was to ask the same question about the song that is asked about any scene in any play: what is it about? What is "If Momma Was Married" about? Two sisters who barely know each other and suspect that their mother is the reason: a start. Not a start for bouncing into a jaunty waltz, though. Well, then ease into it—and Patrick did.

June is the one who is tough on their mother; let her start off with a spoken wish that "if Momma was married . . . [I would be free and happy]." The music begins softly; it's still a three-quarter beat, but it's gentle, unemphatic. Louise repeats June's words over the melody for them, but with a different meaning, which comes clear as she slips into singing the lyric lightly, picking up speed and volume as she goes—and soon it's the same song with a different meaning and consequently sounds altogether different.

But where does the song go? Nowhere, really, since it has no story to tell. Nothing happens, nor is there any emotional development in the lyric for the girls. But a lot has been unearthed in the scene: the sisters have acknowledged there is something missing in their relationship; they have hinted they wish it were otherwise; they have even suggested Rose is what has kept them apart. When you want to take off, suggestions can be wings. The story that made the song a scene didn't have to be imposed, it wasn't pasted on; it was waiting in the characters and their relationship, and it came to life during the song.

At the first notes, the sisters are strangers, miles apart; as they sing, they discover each other through their shared attitude to the Act, draw closer by their feelings about Rose, even closer by the desire to have what each never did: a sister. What ultimately brings them together is laughter, *shared* laughter at Rose's vaudeville Act that has kept them apart. By the last triumphant note, the sisters are sisters who love each other. Every night, the grasp of each other's hand on that last note brought a thunderous roar that stopped the show. "If Momma Was Married" worked.

The second act of *Gypsy* is deceptive and tricky, which may sound redundant but isn't. All but the first scene takes place in the world of burlesque, raising bawdy expectations that are not fulfilled. In this version, the burlesque houses and strippers are tawdry and tired, absent of sex except for Louise's adventure into striptease which turns her into Gypsy Rose Lee, the one glamorous note in the sleazy world around her.

What is tricky is keeping the humor in the scenes without making it jokes-on-demand that sugarcoat the desperate despair that has seeped into Rose's dream. Even trickier is how, once again, to convert entertainment numbers in a musical into scenes in a musical play.

"Together," the first book number in act two, is plainly a vaudeville act aimed at the audience. The three leading players sing jokey lyrics to a jingly tune and hoke it up as performers, not characters, usually with much success. Not this time around, though; this time the players seemed uncomfortable and the song an ill-judged mistake, because what had been brief plot points for Rose and her daughter were now dramatic turning points in the understated battle between them that becomes the clothesline of the second act. The song didn't belong, but it was an audience favorite, it was the centerpiece of the scene, it had to stay. There had to be a way of making it work for the story, and there was. What gentled it into belonging was the way Rose now began it.

Rose often has more than one motivation for what she does. She needs Louise for the act, she needs Herbie for the act, but she also needs them emotionally: she never wants to be alone. This Rose really does want a family. It may not be her first priority, but she wants one. So she starts "Together" sweetly, arm-in-arming Herbie to sit by her, coaxing Louise to sit on her other side. Soon she has them clowning and horsing around with her, enjoying letting loose for the first time. Instead of faithfully reproducing choreographed movement, they screw up some steps and ad-lib others. She has turned them into a family; they *are* a family— mother, father, and daughter having fun together, as the title says.

When the actors give the characters dimension, they give them possibilities which music bolsters. "Together" became constantly improvised fun for the three actors. Each audience felt the fun was improvised just for them at just that moment and fell in love with the family.

"You Gotta Get a Gimmick" almost slipped by. Its purpose in the show is to stop it. It does, and always will, no matter who performs it, how well or how badly. But even in rehearsal, in this production, a showstopper existing solely to be a showstopper was a wrong number. It also derailed the three actresses struggling in the unfamiliar territory of burlesque and strippers to locate characters they could make real, at least to themselves. The number is choreographed for five-six-seven-eight caricatures with no regard for what idiosyncratic character each actress was trying to breathe a little life into.

It was apparent at the first run-through of act two that the damage done by "Gimmick" didn't stop with the number or the strippers. In a musical comedy, a showstopper couldn't have caused damage. In a musical comedy, it's a number that does its job, stops the show, and the show moves happily onward. In a musical play, a showstopper is a number that has nothing to do with the story or the characters and stops the play dead in its tracks no matter how hysterical the audience gets. The show moves on because the scenery moves on. With "Gimmick," just what show was no longer clear: not the show it was meant to be, and certainly not the show we were all so excited about doing.

"Gimmick" tainted everything that took place in the burlesque house. Rehearsing the second act, where the characters are heading for explosion, I was constantly looking for moments to heighten emotionally so that the explosions wouldn't come from nowhere. Emotion has long been out of fashion in the theatre, but for me emotion is synonymous with theatre. The burlesque-dressing-room scenes with only Rose, Herbie, and Louise are packed with emotional moments. They were being acted by Patti, Boyd, and Laura with as much emotional reality as their first-act scenes, but they came off as melodramatic and contrived. Every moment in a play affects every other moment in a ripple effect there is no way to prevent. The show-biz aura of "Gimmick" affected every moment in the burlesque house.

It was my fault. Tempted by the showstopper "Gimmick" would assuredly be, I ignored the effect it was having on what I myself was trying to achieve. There was so much to get done with a whole company as well as the stars and only three weeks to do it in—a valid excuse if any excuse is valid. But none is for failure. The ridiculously short time of three weeks can only be pointed out for the success I hoped this would be.

This wasn't the first instance of my being at fault and for a somewhat similar reason. I had overlooked the damage done by allowing the Farmboys and the Hollywood Blondes to give their customary mindless musical-comedy performances—the boys hoking it up in the hotel room, the Blondes equally hokey in the burlesque house. They had been cast with actors—young, inexperienced, but talented actors. What they deserved was the respect of being treated like actors. I did: I got to work directing them. I encouraged, even prodded them to find characters for themselves and then showed them how with only one or two lines, even with no lines, they could make a marked difference to the show. It really paid off in ways I wouldn't have thought of and was saved taking the time and trouble of inventing. One example: in the hotel room, what had been an anonymous pleasant Farmboy became a smartass, juvenile lecher who made passes at June. The chain of reactions from June, who slapped him, to Rose, who wanted to slap him, to Tulsa, who protected June for a reason we don't find out until the end of the act, made the hotel room alive with active characters instead of a background for the stars and stick figures. A smaller example (for sexual equality): in the Toreadorable number, the vivid enmity between two of the girls comically prevented any semblance of a chorus line—if there was one—and illustrated again how desperate Rose was in casting her net.

"Gimmick," once examined as it should have been, revealed a positive possibility. Rather than making it more difficult for each of the would-be strippers, it could even help them fit in the play if the number itself could fit into the play. But how? How could an unabashed, unapologetic comic turn be converted into a song in a musical play?

Again, ask the basic question: if the strippers weren't singing "You Gotta Get a Gimmick" to stop the show, why *were* they singing it? The answer had always been there if anyone looked beyond the lyric to where the song comes in the play. Tessie has just introduced Louise to Mazeppa and Electra; they are explaining what it takes to be a stripper—well, there it is, without distortion or finagling, a smooth transition to the three battered friends teaching Louise their business of stripping. The difference made simply by having the number sung not out front to the audience but directly to Louise was gratifyingly out of proportion to how much it did for the story, for the three strippers, and eventually for the second act.

For the story, it restored the focus to Louise simply by her listening and reacting to advice illustrated by a bugle blown out between the legs, strategically placed lights, and balletically ferocious bumps. "Simply" is a huge word unless the listener is Laura Benanti, who can listen and react with seeming spontaneity every night as only the finest actresses can.

For the strippers, it gave each of them a relationship with Louise and another with the other two that became the foundation of a character. In the original production of *Gypsy*, the three strippers were youngish, attractive, and sexy; their function was to entertain and be funny. Fifty years later, being funny was still a function, but they were blowsy and over the hill, as they would have been in that end-of-the-line burlesque house. Electra was the easiest to give dimension to, not because her role is the smallest but because the Electra I envisioned was a ladylike alcoholic: completely ossified, dead drunk out of her head, able to put one foot in front of the other only with great difficulty. It's not easy, however, to perform a number that calls for belting and heavy bumping and grinding by barely moving and hardly projecting because you ostensibly are too drunk. Marilyn Caskey's problem was to do less and then less than that, but she brought it off hilariously.

Tessie Tura has presumably surefire laughs and overtly pretentious remarks that had been difficult for Alison Fraser to use to create a character she believed in. Now it all came together: Tessie became a remnant in a sagging world. Tough and fragile, she was moving and funny because she wasn't working to be either. She was just Tessie Tura, the unfortunate Texas Twirler.

Mazeppa really worked only in the first production because her bugle routine as a gladiator was originally done in a nightclub act by Faith Dane, which she more or less reproduced in the first *Gypsy*. Since the routine was essentially hers, Faith was comfortable as the helmeted Rambo Woman she played. Her successors were uncomfortable, unintentionally coming out as cartoon lesbians; but they brought the house down with the bugle bit, so what the hell?

Nancy Opel, who was a terrific Miss Cratchitt in act one, learned to play a good bugle but was uncomfortable and not very good as Mazeppa until we reworked "Gimmick." When Lenora Nemetz replaced her in the Broadway company, because Nancy unfortunately was committed elsewhere, I made life easier for her by replacing Mazeppa and her Gladiator Ballet with Mazeppa and her Revolution Ballet. This season it was the American Revolution: Mazeppa wore a Paul Revere tricorn and red, white, and blue in strategic places. Lenora was also a terrific Cratchitt, from the moment she walked her Cratchitt walk across the stage.

Nancy didn't have the advantage of playing a patriotic stripper; but no longer hampered by gladiator choreography, her Mazeppa became sarcastic, not strident; friendly, not fierce; and inventively funny with her technical explanation of the limitations of having "no talent." The Rambo-like military stomping was excised from her solo.

This and other changes I made in the choreography did not make life easy for Bonnie Walker. No one can reproduce the

Jerome Robbins choreography for *Gypsy* as meticulously as Bonnie. She has always done it, and she and I have always worked like Burns and Allen. But choreography is more than steps, and I had been making other, small changes. Kids fell down or fought with each other in the vaudeville acts to show that Rose snapped up whatever bodies she could get; in the barnyard number, June— Leigh Ann Larkin, as tough a customer as Rose yet coruscatingly funny—was sarcastically and humorously aware of the cliché "Moo Cow" song to show she knew how bad the act was; Louise had a larger would-be dancing role in "All I Need Is the Girl" to keep the focus more on her. Bonnie, rehearsing these numbers, was unsure whether the actors were fighting her or obeying me. She wants so much to please, even the dead Jerry Robbins; her nerves were jangling. Belatedly, I explained what I had been learning in big dollops as I went along: when you have a different vision, *everything* has to conform or nothing seems right.

"Gimmick" and Tessie and her colleagues now conformed to my vision, they were now an integral part of the story, and that made a remarkable difference to the second act. In its other versions, it had always been considered just a notch below the first act; now, for the first time, it was raised to its level. The taint of melodrama and glitz had been removed. It had as much emotional intensity, if not more, because its scenes went deeper and carried more weight. Totally unexpected.

There was one factor above all others that made this *Gypsy* extraordinary. Roll your eyes if you will, but the production was driven by love, beginning with Tom. That was what had made him urge me to do the show with Patti. Mine for him made me determined this *Gypsy* wasn't going to be like any *Gypsy* I or anyone else had directed before. When he died, loss told me more about love than I had ever known. For me, nothing in life is more important. Nothing in this production was more important.

Gypsy was always about the need for recognition—which is also a need for love of one kind or another. It reaches its climax in the very last scene of the play, between Rose and Louise, when Rose admits she did it all for herself and then answers why:

"Just wanted to be noticed," she says.

"Like I wanted you to notice me," says her daughter—meaning "Like I wanted you to love me." *Wanted,* past tense; and Rose, the no-longer-wanted mother, breaks down in tears.

Love was always the subject; it just needed a spotlight.

Love for *Gypsy* was shared by everyone in the rehearsal hall. Not the love the company had when it arrived—the love of the show as a favorite musical. Once we began work around the table, discovering there was so much more to be mined than they had suspected, the actors fell in love with *Gypsy*—really in love. That made the work better, and *that* made *them* better. Not just this player or that—everyone. And the better they got, the more they loved what they were doing; and the more they loved their work, the better the whole show got and continued to get, until the first audience told us it was even better than we had thought.

Love was driving everything. I'd never been happier in rehearsal, because of the mutual love affair with the company. It began, as it had to, with Patti—a lightning journey from testing each other the first day to mutual trust and enjoyment of each other by the third. Seeing that, Boyd and Laura came along, the others followed like groupies, and the rehearsal hall was suffused with love that transformed the time and the place and the work. When the company moved into the theatre, that love flooded the stage, poured over the footlights into the audience, which bathed in it and sent back waves of its own night after night until the night it wouldn't go home.

How could that *Gypsy* not be extraordinary?

The City Center run was limited to three weeks, the first of which was largely previews. The adulation excited during those three short weeks paled beside the citywide love affair after it closed. Only a ticker-tape parade was lacking. I might even have begun to believe I was really that good, but I left for Quogue immediately after closing night to prepare Tom's memorial.

It was to be on August 24, his birthday and our anniversary, under a tent in his park—*his* park because he had turned acres of what had been a dark jungle of trees strangled with bittersweet into the most serene place on the planet. What he called "rooms" were small areas of variegated plants and shrubs and flowers separated by sunlit corridors formed by so many different trees: birch, maple, evergreen, tulip, and the sequentially blossoming fruit trees—pear, cherry, apple. The park was what he created, year after year; the summer day of his memorial was so perfect he must have created it, too. He had to have been there; he *was* there. All the people who spoke felt his presence; all the people who strolled through the "rooms" after the ceremony to discover more of him felt they saw him as I remembered him: wearing his torn straw hat to shield his fair skin while riding his lawn mower around his park. There was no mention of *Gypsy* at the memorial other than the presence of three friends who had been involved with it at one time or another: Bernadette Peters, Tyne Daly, and Scott Rudin. But it had come into my mind at an odd moment for an odd reason.

When I spoke at the memorial, I held on to the tent pole the way I later held on to the proscenium of the St. James when I spoke at the invitation dress rehearsal. I looked at ease, but I was holding on in both cases, because my legs were shaking badly. At the St. James, they were shaking because I was embarrassed by the prolonged applause when I came on stage. At the memorial, they were shaking because even though I believed what I said—that he was there in the park and his spirit always would be—at that moment, I missed his physical presence so badly I literally couldn't stand it.

After City Center, London with Patti had been the plan, but no acceptable theatre was available for at least a year. No one seemed to care. The excitement at home in New York had turned everyone's eyes toward Broadway. Surprise? Hardly. No matter what the artistic level of Broadway, it is always the goal, the prize, the brass ring on the merry-go-round. Everyone in the theatre community said *Gypsy* belonged on Broadway; it had to go to Broadway *now* to show the audience what theatre can be. Producers were ready; theatres were offered; the company was available and half out of its head with desire. But there was a catch. In this world, obviously there would be, and obviously it would be money. The financing wasn't there—for one equally obvious, time-honored reason:

Considered a summer production, the show had not been reviewed by the magazines, but the newspapers that did offered unanimous raves for the show. And were ecstatic about Patti's passionate, risky performance. But not unanimously: the exception was the *New York Times*. In the event that a *Times* reader didn't believe in reading reviews, the paper put its reservation about her in a big headline over the review. Complain if you will, as you will, about the power of the *Times,* or claim it doesn't have the power it once did, the belief in the New York theatre is that no show can survive a negative review from the *New York Times*. It doesn't matter if that's true; it doesn't matter that exceptions can be found. What does matter is that investors in shows believe it's true, and theirs is the power to put a show on Broadway or keep it off. Protest; argue how word of mouth can bring them in, and just listen to the buzz about *Gypsy*—listen to descriptions of its audiences literally shouting and screaming throughout the show every night, standing up every night at the end of Patti's "Rose's Turn"—but (forgive the interruption) did you see Brantley's review?

Nothing revealed more how Tom's death had changed my perspective on the theatre and on what mattered in life than my reaction to the fevered speculation over Broadway for *Gypsy*. I didn't care about going to Broadway. I had done what Tom wanted me to do, and I had accomplished what I wanted to accomplish. Well, not entirely: Patti still hadn't fully realized her potential, although you'd never have known it from the hysteria she caused in the audience. *Gypsy* as a show, however, had been the event I promised it would be—bigger, actually, than anyone's dream. I was proud how well my work was received; that was enough for me. I didn't need money or Broadway's validation.

And there had been a lovely bonus: my relationship with Patti. A piece of paper couldn't come between us. She was on the road, doing concerts on what she called her Pay-Off-the-Debts Tour. We e-mailed constantly, her notes always asking, "Any news about us on Broadway?" The designers called now and then. They had counted on London to finally bring some money for their work. That work had been even harder than it would have been in a Broadway production, because they had to spend so much time and call in so many chips to make magical bricks out of discount straw. They didn't ask about Broadway, but I knew. To the actors who had never been on Broadway, some of them never even been in a show, Broadway was an impossible dream, but they dreamed it anyway and I knew. The actors who were not neophytes but had never had parts this good and had never been as good—I knew. But when Patti had to face that not only were dreams of going to Broadway gone but hope was gone, *Gypsy* was not going to Broadway or anywhere else, she was devastated, and I didn't want to know that. Patti LuPone is a raw life force; she must not be devastated. But she was. It was awful to behold, and I couldn't. So I went to work to get *Gypsy* on Broadway, even though I thought of Broadway as Chernobyl.

Among the small group of producers who had contributed enhancement money for the show at City Center and who were supposed to do it in London, there was one who was quietly passionate about theatre—what he himself thought was theatre, not necessarily what he was told was theatre. No nuance of this production of *Gypsy* escaped him; he loved it unequivocally. He was also the most likely to take a risk for what he believed in, the most likely to have the lottery number that could get *Gypsy* to Broadway. Uniquely, he was a producer you could trust. As anyone active in the theatre reading this already knows, his name is Roger Berlind. Roger is responsible for *Gypsy* playing on Broadway. I promised him and all the producers that I would make the *New York Times* change its mind about Patti LuPone. It's what critics praise, not what they pan, that antagonizes and depresses the theatre community. Even *Hamlet* has flaws. I wasn't just pitching the producers when I said I could make the *Times* change its mind; I believed it, and I believed I could because I agreed with the objections.

If I had admitted that to anyone, I would have been stoned; but to know what is wrong, even just to think you know, makes it easier to get it right.

The hardest thing to get in New York is a theatre for a musical. We had the St. James, where I had done *Gypsy* with Tyne Daly in 1989—a good omen. But during the time it took to get the financing, we lost the St. James. The breath-holding period during which a London transfer seemed set to supplant us took its toll on Patti. When the St. James was once again ours, solidly this time, her relief was too enormous. Patti LuPone, Star, made her appearance with a litany of complaints and demands. I didn't want to face rehearsals for a Chernobyl venue with a diva, however talented. I invited her to dinner.

"What's wrong?" she asked, her antennae out. Oh, she knew me and she knew herself.

Part of being a director is being a therapist. Patti's diva behavior stemmed from student days at Juilliard, when she felt her talent wasn't given the full recognition it deserved because she didn't look like the conventional idea of a leading lady. Even a nontherapist would know it dated farther back than that, but Juilliard is as far back as I'm going.

Dinner was at a table in the window of Chez Josephine on Forty-second Street's Theatre Row, rain really slamming down outside. A long hug—we were genuinely glad to be together again—hello-hello with the owner from both of us, drinks ordered and served, and then a conversation that was largely a monologue from me:

Her complaints and demands were her prerogative as a star. I had worked with many stars; stars didn't interest me. Artists interested me, and she was one of the few artists in musical theatre. When she was the artist, I loved working with her; it excited me, it inspired me, it got cylinders firing that hadn't fired in years. This was why Tom wanted me to do *Gypsy* with her. Behind her demands, one—that there be no opening night on Broadway—exposed the fear behind almost all: the *New York Times.* She felt the *Times* had never really liked her, she was sure it never would; she didn't want to experience that pain again. She wouldn't, I said. No? No. Why was I so sure? Because I was sure I knew how to get the *Times* to change its mind about her.

Patti LuPone is not very trusting, but she trusted me. She believed I could make the *Times* change its opinion of her. Why she did, I have no idea. It may have helped when I told her it had been my goal that she fulfill her potential and admitted I'd failed.

"Not this time," I said.

At that moment, we were sitting at our table in the window, which was apart from the other diners, and the rain outside was coming down so hard we couldn't see or be seen through it. The privacy made us feel as though we were in what used to be called a "love nest." We both relaxed, and I stopped worrying about the diva. She was gone.

The first mistake at City Center that had to be corrected had been mine. Her wig was unattractive, and since there hadn't been time to make a new one, I had asked her to wear her own hair. Without hesitation: "Okay." The result was she looked like Patti LuPone, familiar star, not Rose, stage mother from hell. A big mistake. I admitted it was mine and apologized. A wig this time. The suggestion made her as happy as a child and receptive to what was next:

The Jocko scene is really a prologue to the play whose first scene and song in the kitchen either shoot Rose out into orbit or start her out on a wrong foot from which she can only partly recover, no matter how great her "Rose's Turn" is. At City Center, she had started off on the wrong foot. Patti LuPone knows how to deliver a song, and her audience goes wild at the first high note. The screaming and shouting made it easy for me to pretend all was fine and dandy—but it wasn't.

That summary of the situation didn't throw her; it wasn't entirely news. Over the months since City Center, she herself had figured there was something wrong in the beginning; she even knew it was the way she was doing "Some People." But what was the right way? How should she do it? With Rose-like energy, yes, fine, sure; but where would the energy come from? Not anger. She didn't want to play an angry Rose all night long. Nor did I want her to. Granted, anger was always raging underneath, but it had to be kept there except at chosen moments—as when June leaves and the boys think the act is washed up.

A director should never bring up a problem without being sure of the answer. If not anger, then what was the source of the energy needed?

"Joy."

That caught her; I explained. The world can be content to sit on its ass, but not Rose. Rose wants to travel in her mother's footsteps: go places, do things, get herself noticed. She's on a high when she brings her kids back home to the kitchen. Not angry at Jocko, she's finished with him, happy because she's moving on as directed by one of her dreams—a new act for her beloved Baby June. They're going to get out of Seattle and conquer the world via the Orpheum Circuit. This Rose is a dynamo who's taking life by the tail and laughs.

Patti latched on. Her Rose was going to be fun.

Her second big song, "Everything's Coming Up Roses," also had to be rethought and redone, from the first line of the speech leading into it. She had started out racing through that speech, through the song itself, slowing down only for the coda, where she used all the vocal power she had and finished to cheers as the first-act curtain came down. As Rose herself says, "If you have a good, strong finish, they'll forgive you for anything."

Not everybody. Barbara Cook, an old friend who arguably knows more about singing theatre songs than anyone else, had seen *Gypsy* at City Center. She too felt Patti had a potential she hadn't yet fulfilled.

"Why do you think that is, Barbara?"

"She goes too fast."

Validation from Barbara Cook. Did I need it? Who doesn't have insecurity? Recently, I told Patti she was racing and rattling again.

She grinned. "I've been told that my whole career."

The grin was a happy one because Patti is an actress who always wants her director, if she trusts him—if she doesn't, he's her nanny—to come back to her dressing room and give her notes.

"The crazy thing is, I don't know I'm rattling. I have to be told." The next performance, the rattling was gone. She was exhilarated: slowing down had helped her find a new moment in the scene. She loves finding new moments.

That's how it works when the theatre is in yesteryear hands: during the run of a show, the director checks the performance regularly and the actor is still at work exploring the role.

With "Roses," Patti knew the reason she was racing was that she was unsure what Rose was feeling and where she was heading. Even with her racing, the notes she hit were full-throated and glorious and the curtain came down to insanely thunderous applause. Who could ask for more? Well, *I* was now, and now I had to break down the speech and the song for her. She interrupted: she wanted to explain how she worked as an actor, because she thought it would help me with her. It did. That explanation changed our relationship, professionally and personally.

"I'm not stupid, I'm just slow," she said.

I always hear her saying that. It's pure Patti LuPone. Other actors wouldn't go straight to that point. As close as we had become, she brought us closer by exposing herself, telling me in effect how to get to her, telling me what she needed to know to play a scene as I wanted, as *she* wanted, ultimately as we both wanted. That trust was the foundation of an enduring relationship that couldn't be categorized. Working together was and is an endlessly creative joy.

The tone for a song is very often set by a speech leading into the song; the tone for the speech is set before a word is spoken by what's going on inside the character. That's axiomatic, but it's too often ignored.

The second of Rose's big, defining numbers starts with her lead-in speech; the tone for that speech is set by her internal reaction to the letter she is reading on a railway-station bench—a letter from her daughter June, her star, her bread and butter, a letter telling Rose the act was never any good, she was never any good, she isn't needed anymore, she's nothing. At first, Rose is stunned and bewildered; then shock turns to anger and simmers to a boil as she speaks until she is ready to kill. Kill she does, and as she does, her need for revenge right now, this minute, shatters all sense. She goes around the bend and we have a temporarily crazy woman singing and believing "Everything's Coming Up Roses."

That's how I laid it out for Patti. She had ideas of her own; they were tried, some incorporated, some not. But we knew where *Rose* had to go and that Patti would get her there. As she warned, she was slow. But once she got it in her gut and in her head, she had both the emotional electricity and the vocal dynamics to make the song chilling and thrill the audience every night so that they screamed as though on cue as the first-act curtain came down.

Even the *New York Times* was knocked out by the "Rose's Turn" she did at City Center. The third and last of Rose's big numbers, it invariably got a huge standing ovation from an audience of over two thousand—from the high-powered in the expensive, uncomfortable orchestra to Patti's fans in the cheaper, equally uncomfortable rear mezzanine and gallery. The last section of the song was particularly overwhelming. Boosted by a series of remarkable lighting effects by Howell Binkley, she tore savagely into those "For me! For me!"s, making a spectacular ending that was a catharsis for everyone. Nevertheless, I thought what she was doing was a collage that didn't really suit her, and that she could do much better; I wanted to do a new "Rose's Turn" for her.

"Rose's Turn" is divided into three sections, the first designed to rock the house by having the star playing Rose shout out "Here she is, boys! Here she is, world! Here's Rose!" as the intro to a down-and-dirty version of a striptease, bumping and grinding as though to the manner born. From Merman on, every Rose scored in that segment, with one exception: Patti LuPone. She was uncomfortable trying to perform a version of the strip as her predecessors, each in her own distinctive style, had done to the delight of the audience wanting to see the equivalent of a star's underwear. There was no style that suited Patti. She was awkward and tentative; she didn't take to choreographed movement, thus she wasn't very good at it—or vice versa. She tried—Patti LuPone will always try—and Bonnie, who never gives up on anyone, smiled and cajoled and encouraged with makeshift adjustments. I put in my two or three cents. A collage, as I said, was the result: more than presentable, and Patti more than just got through the section. But what sufficed at City Center wouldn't at the St. James—not because it was for Broadway but because of what had happened to Patti's Rose.

The new opening kitchen scene feeding a new "Some People"

gave Rose new dimensions, as did the new act-ending railway-station speech catapulting her into a furious, frightening new "Everything's Coming Up Roses." Patti LuPone, star performer, had metamorphosed into a mesmerizing Rose in a dazzling coat of many colors. That was the Rose I wanted in "Rose's Turn."

We had been doing the number more or less as it always had been done. Why not? It was the landmark eleven o'clock number of musical theatre. I hadn't given a thought to re-examining it as I had every other number in the show. Would I find something new if I did? Something deeper, richer—something Patti could use to make a "Rose's Turn" that was all her own as she had made the other numbers her own?

I also didn't think her City Center "Rose's Turn" was good enough for this new *Gypsy* we were finding in rehearsal for Broadway, of all places. We sat around the table again, this time in a very streamlined rehearsal studio with big windows overlooking over-bulbed and overcrowded Forty-second Street. The show was becoming even more extraordinary for Broadway than it had been at the relatively Off-Broadway City Center. The irony was lost on me, I was too wrapped up in the work, bursting with ideas coming from God knows where or why. Perhaps compensation for the loss of Tom, but the standard Higher Power would only compensate someone in a stratosphere of clouds and feathery wings. I was ninety years old, and maybe I was aging backwards, but my sole memory problem was trying to remember when I last had been so creative.

A visual very often provides my impetus. With "If Momma Was Married," it was Louise's hand held out to June. Re-examining "Rose's Turn," it was an image of Rose in the paint-smeared smock she wore in all the backstages of her life. She was saying "Here's Rose," but she wasn't ripping the smock open to reveal that red strip dress because she wasn't going to do a strip then. Her "Here's Rose" was *mocking* the whole notion. That broke the mold the number had been frozen in. I asked questions that hadn't existed before. Since Rose had ridiculed Louise as "a cheap stripper," why would she do a strip herself? Obviously, she has to take a pass at doing one or reference it some way; that's how the number is written. But how would she really feel about doing it?

When she angrily prowls the empty stage outside the star dressing room of the daughter who has no use for her, she rages: "I was born too soon and started too late!"—otherwise "I could have been better than any of you!"

A better stripper? Is that what Patti LuPone's Rose would mean? Her Rose is bigger; her Rose wants more, wants bigger, wants the world! She has contempt for burlesque; she sneers at it and at Louise when she says: "Here she is, boys!" When she snarls "Here she is, world!," the grandiosity of addressing the "world" tells us she's lost reality. "Here's *Rose!*" *That's* what she's been getting to: *Rose!* In lights—big, bright lights! *Rose* demanding to be looked at and seen because she is finally, at very long last, the Star she was always meant to be. That madness Patti LuPone could play with frightening intensity at different levels at will. And boy, did she!

When the music changes for the strip, Rose switches in a flash to a sexual smile—of course she's sexy, no one's sexier—and opens the smock like a stripper, revealing that red dress. "Play it, boys!" she commands, and when she asks if they like what she shows them, the answering "Yes!" is from the whole world. She smiles and nods with disdain: of course they like it, *she's* got it. And then—candy for Patti—she switches again:

Starting like June with "Hello, everybody! My name's"—June's gone, fury is back—*"Rose!"* That harsh "Rose" is a reminder of who commands the attention around here; but the next minute, the star is gone and she's a girl laughing, a little mad, joking, playing games, flirting sexually, reveling in letting loose any way she can think of, letting go—but the phrase "let go" trips her up, ends her frenzied joy, begins a downward spiral that yanks her back to Louise telling her mother she has got to "let go of [her]!" Once again, Rose is not needed; once again a daughter is lost. When June left, Rose was furious, but she could go on, she could start a new act. Without Louise, there's no place to go; she can do nothing, is nothing. Then why did she do it all? What did it get her?

Everything changes: music, lights, setting, Rose. Self-examination turns "Rose's Turn" into an encapsulation of Rose's whole frustrated, angry life, which produces a breakdown, sending her completely over the edge. This is a "Rose's Turn" that uses everything Patti LuPone can dig up and keep digging into the longer she plays it; a "Rose's Turn" that everybody, without exception, stands up and cheers. You have to.

When Rose gets richer, the other characters get richer and *Gypsy* gets richer. In this production, where all the actors interact with Rose to some degree, Patti couldn't change without every other actor changing—from Jim Bracchitta, both in the Jocko scene and in the burlesque house, to Sami Gayle and Bill Raymond in the kitchen scene, to Leigh Ann Larkin and Pearce Wegener in the hotel room, to Alison Fraser in the burlesque house, to the Farm-boys, the Toreadorables, to every single member of the company, because it's a company of *actors*. As at City Center, work was done regularly sitting around a table; the company, being that company, heard, saw and *felt* what was happening to Patti and Boyd, to Patti and Laura, to Laura and Boyd. By second nature now, they dug deeper again, found more, invented more.

It didn't seem that Laura and Tony Yazbeck could improve on their scene built around "All I Need Is the Girl," but they did. It now existed on two levels, the literal and the metaphorical. The dream he ached for was for more than a girl—and enhanced immeasurably by her dream to be worthy of him. Everyone dreams for something; the number was now for everyone. Everyone hoping that Louise would get what she was yearning for had always been there, but Laura's yearning made the scene and song more moving—which hadn't seemed possible.

The biggest change in her performance came from something seemingly unconnected: Patti's new bows after "Rose's Turn." Her bows had been done in a fashion gauged to bring off the trick devised so many years ago in London for Angela Lansbury. Those bows, however, were done by Angela as Rose and later by Tyne Daly as Rose. Patti's bows were done by Patti LuPone, Star—that's who bowed at City Center. This new Rose had to bow differently. What is such a great delight and so rewarding about working with Patti LuPone is that when she's challenged—in this case, to bow as *her* Rose would bow after having the triumph she believed she has deserved her whole life—she comes up with bows that are original, dazzling, funny, touching, and always true to the character.

Those bows took us directly into another change I was after: playing the final scene between mother and daughter to make it clearly the climax of the whole play, as was always intended.

The first line of the scene that follows the bows starts with a laugh because of the mood those demented bows have established. That laugh gives the illusion that the relationship between mother and daughter is in fine shape. Rose seems in control even with Louise gone and replaced by Gypsy Rose Lee, a powerful, glamorous woman. A bit distant, she's not threatening; she seems pleasant, amused by Rose's antics. It isn't too difficult for Rose to admit to her she did do everything for herself. But Rose's admission unintentionally changes the tone of the scene, for it has a profound effect on her daughter. When she asks "*Why*, Mother?," it's Louise asking.

"Just wanted to be noticed," Rose says, trying to make light of it.

When Louise, on the edge of tears, says, "Like I wanted you to notice me?," meaning "Like I wanted you to love me," we are at the climax of the evening. The point of *Gypsy* is made. What greater need for recognition is there than the need of the child for love from the parent?

For the first time in her life, Rose faces what she has done to her daughter. Her horror that she completely failed her child destroys her. For the first time in the play, Rose is vulnerable: she cries. With Patti, it's a frighteningly believable breakdown that makes Rose a pitiable figure. Gypsy, who has made peace with what Rose put her through, says, "It's okay, Mother." Then, seeing what the woman she feared for most of her life is reduced to, walks over to her to comfort her and says, "It's okay, Rose." Daughter has become mother.

Not for very long, though. Rose wasn't made to be an underdog of any kind. She chokes back her sobs, wipes away the tears, and is back in control, making jokes and conning Louise in style. Oh, she makes a small concession when she senses Louise might not be buying; but poor Rose!—what she doesn't sense or won't see is that it isn't Louise who is or isn't buying. Louise is gone permanently. Children leave their parents. It's Gypsy Rose Lee who walks away from Rose, laughing at Rose unchanged, still being Rose. Gypsy will take her mother to the party, she'll take care of her materially; but she's free of her—which is why she can laugh at Rose still trying to con her. Laura Benanti's amused laugh as Gypsy, not Louise, walks away was one of the memorable moments of the performance.

It wasn't easy for Laura to do this. Her emotions are very close to the surface and she is extremely compassionate. Patti's breakdown affected her so much, she was in tears herself. She knew it was wrong—it was hard for her to kill the feeling—but she is an actress. She battled herself; an encouraging push and she gave a performance of Louise-into-Gypsy no one ever had before. It came to a head in the scene in Gypsy's dressing room where the two women have a knock-down-drag-out. It is now a shattering high point of the show because of two superb actresses at their best.

Some particulars change from night to night, but the scene is always a killer. It's not easy for Laura to tell off someone she cares about. She does it, though, and at the peak, her body is trembling so much, she has to hold on to the dressing table to hold on to herself. Some nights, the toll it takes has her in tears; to stop them and get herself back into the toughness of Gypsy Rose Lee, she will slam her hand down on the table. But she is always Gypsy, it's always done honestly, and she is always grateful that she's playing the scene with Patti LuPone, who thrives on challenge so long as it's honest. Going all out in that scene is why Laura can play the last scene and play it with enormous subtlety.

All of this and more developed in the rehearsal studio that for three weeks was ours. The big windows overlooked a Forty-second Street that was out of sight and mind; the security guards at the desk downstairs didn't ask for passes; dozens of backpacks had unassigned permanent places behind the line of production tables, and I was on creative speed. Three weeks! The whole City Center production, from rehearsal to opening night, was done in three weeks. On that memorable closing night, I had a fresh look at the show—if you can call coming back after not seeing three performances a fresh look. The intensity of anticipation in the crowd in front of the theatre, in the lobby, in the aisles before the performance was startling. Merely lowering the house lights brought pandemonium, and the performance didn't disappoint. I sat there, swept along with the audience, marveling at what was on the stage. But even then, the cold eye I can never close when watching my own work was seeing what I hadn't until then: missed moments, some of them big, that needed work, to put it politely. Unfinished work is never finished; happily, though, evidenced by this performance, the work that had been done had taken the show farther than I dreamed. Now it was over; the show was closing. I stowed the moments in my attic and gave myself to enjoying the night.

But it didn't close. We went back into rehearsal; the unfinished work was finished; new moments, big and small, were changed and invented. Now we were ready for the new work to be seen.

The producers had taken a financial risk in bringing *Gypsy* back to Broadway less than five years after the Mendes version. I invited them first to the run-through in the rehearsal studio before we moved into the theatre. The note in my journal for that day reads:

"Run-through. Producers, designers and John. [John was John Barlow, *Gypsy*'s press representative who is obsessed with musicals but backs it up by knowing more about musicals than almost anyone professionally connected to them or anyone who writes about them professionally.] All thrilled. Steve also there. Well, Steve."

Translation: with the exception of Steve, everyone at the run-through was flabbergasted, dazzled, amazed—not only that the performance was richer and so much deeper than it had been at City Center but that it was even possible to be richer and go deeper. John hugged me, shook his head, and said, "What you've done is incredible!" I held that in my head all during Steve.

Steve, of course, is Stephen Sondheim, never exactly bursting with enthusiasm for *Gypsy*—even less for *West Side Story.* Understandable: he wrote only lyrics for those two shows; his enthusiasm, his caring is for all the shows he wrote the music for as well. He had liked the production at City Center, with reservations. Perhaps affected by a room reverberating with acclaim, he liked the new *Gypsy* a little better, also with reservations.

When a musical moves from the rehearsal hall to the theatre, the director warns the company to be prepared for the performance to fall apart. With *Gypsy*, no one was prepared for the total screw-up by the self-styled Technical Director. At City Center, the few pieces of minimalist scenery—doors, for example—were moved by actors or stagehands. At Broadway's St. James Theatre, the doors were automated. That meant they came on when and where they weren't supposed to and couldn't be stopped. The party line is that computerized automation may take a little longer to get the moves right, but once they are, they're set for the run of the show. Really? Have you ever heard of a computer that didn't break down?

That wasn't the worst problem. The stage-left curtain swags that were part of the portal would suddenly sway as though wind-blown and bang into the ROSE sign, sometimes so hard that a bulb from the sign would crash on stage and break. One night during previews, four bulbs came crashing down as the curtain went up on the second act with Patti on stage. Not missing a line, she got a broom from off stage and managed to sweep off all the broken glass before Laura and the Toreadorables had to get down on the floor for their number. An uninhibited delight, Patti LuPone: the star as cleaning lady.

But what caused the curtains to sway? By the time that had been solved thanks to Paul Libin, the caring man who runs the St. James, the Technical Director had been replaced and all was fine—almost. The host of stage problems had prevented us from getting through the whole show without stopping and ohmygod, here it was, dress rehearsal for our first Broadway audience.

The audience for that dress is invited, which means it's not a real audience, which means that while the actors are nervous, they're hopped up on adrenaline. They know the audience is largely fans and friends plus a few—inevitable on Broadway—schadenfreuders. Many in the invited audience that night had seen the City Center *Gypsy* at least once. They weren't prepared for what they saw at the St. James; I was less prepared for how they reacted. The response to the new tone set by the new Rose Patti played in the kitchen scene and her "Some People" was wild enthusiasm; it kept getting wilder and wilder until the cumulative effect of the battle in Gypsy's dressing room, "Rose's Turn," the bows, and the new last scene blew the roof off the theatre.

That wasn't a real audience, however. The next night was our first preview. People were paying; there were the LuPonistas, of course, but it could be considered close to a real audience. The roof was blown off early—they got this was a new Rose and they went mad for her—and the roof stayed off. All during the previews, we kept rehearsing; we even got back to that table. There were small changes that had a big effect. As fine as Boyd Gaines's Herbie had been, as much as he had held the play together, he had not been quite equal to Rose and Louise and as layered a character as they were until the previews. Then all the subtleties in his performance—Herbie's relationship to the daughter he wanted and the woman he loved—became clear and so strong and affecting that the audience burst into applause mid-scene. Most important of all, Herbie was finally aware of who he was and what he needed, and that changed the course of the second act.

The scenes in the burlesque dressing room shared by the three characters in various combinations had become moments strung together. The line wasn't clear; finessing an unclear moment was frequent; there seemed to be unnecessary repetition. As director, I had to face that the way the characters and their relationships had developed, the play as written didn't always work. The solution was to play against the text in places. Fortunately, the director knew the author, and the author knew how to play against the text and where it would help. Together, they brought it off. The play finally came triumphantly together without any moments I couldn't look at. We were ready for the critics just in time.

The producers didn't quite agree. They were extremely pleased with the production and said so over and over, each of them, all of them, but they weren't exactly mad about the new ending. Jack Viertel, speaking for all of them, sent a long e-mail. It was carefully thought out and written, highly complimentary about the book of *Gypsy,* but mistakenly singled out Rose's admission that she had done everything for herself as the climactic moment which justified mother and daughter walking off together to end the play. This was what they did in 1959, but not in 1989; it was impossible for them to do now. The climax, as I said above, comes with Louise saying "Like I wanted you to notice me?" and Rose's consequent breakdown. Once the truth is exposed, it can't be pushed back in the closet. Rose tries to play Louise as she always has, but she can't, because Louise is gone. Her customary con game is merely amusing to the Gypsy Rose Lee who walks away laughing. It's devastating to Rose. Once again, she is being walked out on. For an uncharacteristic moment, she's down—but only for a moment. What keeps her going is what has always kept her going: her dream. And there it is in big, bright lights: ROSE! Her life; she reaches up for it, the lights start to flicker out one by one, but she chases after them to stop them from going out. She reaches up for them; as the curtain comes down, she still is reaching—she always will be.

That's the ending. It's the only true ending and I kept it. This *Gypsy* is the first to attract a young audience. The ending is one of the first things they talk about. They didn't expect an ending that true in Broadway theatre.

The call came while I was getting dressed for opening night. "You can't repeat this or someone will get fired," the friend said. "Ben Brantley is a rave for Patti and the whole show."

A moment of pure, uncomplicated joy. The *New York Times* had actually changed its opinion of Patti LuPone in print. She had finally fulfilled her potential. The *Times* rave wasn't only for her; it was for Boyd and Laura and Leigh Ann and Tony, for the whole company and what I had achieved with them. The holy effulgence shone on this new *Gypsy*. Proud? Very.

As I went uptown to the theatre, question followed question: Should I tell Patti before the show? Wouldn't she then give the greatest opening-night performance of her life? *Could* I tell her? Hadn't I been asked not to tell anyone? Or was it just not to tell anyone who would repeat it?

I walked into Patti's dressing room. Only she and Matt, her husband, were there, both running higher-than-normal opening-night temperatures. She looked so small next to him. Matt Johnston is big, a big, handsome guy I had become very fond of. He was more nervous, more frightened, more worried, more everything he wouldn't be if he knew what I knew. Patti would look taller; she would be taller. I told them.

"You can't repeat this to anyone," I said, and repeated what I had been told about Brantley's review. Patti's eyes flooded with relief. She held out her arms and we hugged for so much that was unsaid and didn't have to be said until much later when you relive and keep reliving every moment you never really thought would happen.

Matt was in a very different place. "Did you read it?" he demanded.

"No, but the person who—"

"If you didn't see it, we don't know it's true!" He was passionate.

"Matt—" both Patti and I began. But the stakes were higher for him than for anyone in that room. "Unless we see it, we can't be sure."

He had lived through her getting hurt before. He was terrified she would be hurt again and he couldn't face the thought. That's love.

The newspapers were unanimous raves for Patti and the show. The weeklies were even better. The box office brought hope to the producers. Work hasn't stopped on the performance, and won't. Patti calls her performance "a work in progress"; I regularly have rehearsals around a table, and the company loves them. The show is a rare experience, certainly in this theatre in this day: it's loved.

About a month after we opened came another prized e-mail from Mike Nichols. This time, Tom read it with me.

FOUR

How To

I N THE THEATRE, billing is more important than money and power is more important than either, because it begets both. When the director of a musical is also the choreographer, his power is absolute; the show is totally in his hands. Or so it would seem if the hands belonged to Jerome Robbins. But what if the producer was of a dying breed? What if he was notoriously intimidating, if his name was David Merrick and his nickname the "Abominable Showman"? Trouble in River City. And Merrick wasn't even the sole producer of *Gypsy;* he was co-producer with Leland Hayward.

Hayward-Merrick was a marriage of convenience: each had a property the other wanted. Hayward wanted the rights to Gypsy Rose Lee's autobiography, owned by Merrick; Merrick wanted the rights to Jerome Robbins, owned by Hayward. Merrick wanted Jerry because he was the pre-eminent director/choreographer and, subtextually, because Jerome Robbins was the touch of class David Merrick wanted. Both producers wanted me to write the book— which gave me the power, but only until I decided whether I would or wouldn't. Merrick wanted me because the established stalwarts Betty Comden and Adolph Green had come a cropper trying to write about Gypsy Rose Lee whereas I had just come off *West Side Story.* Never mind that the author of the book of a musical about love destroyed by the bigotry and violence of gangs wasn't exactly type casting for the author of the book of a musical about the striptease queen of America. *West Side Story,* however, had been an artistic success, giving me a touch of that class Merrick wanted so badly. Hayward's reason was much simpler: he wanted me to write the book because Jerry wouldn't do the show unless I did.

Jerry's insistence on me was an insight into how he functioned as a director. We had begun *West Side Story* close friends; we ended barely speaking. He couldn't have cared less—I was his choice to write *Gypsy.* Ironically, the show I wrote was not the show he envisioned. He complained that it was *my* show, not his; still, it was a success and he accepted due credit—not as much as he hungered for, but the world of entertainment is crowded with the insatiable who can't receive all the credit they hunger for, because it doesn't exist.

With the occasional exception, the most successful directors don't allow personal relationships to get in their determined way. Jerry, as director, preferred repeat collaborators like Betty Comden and Adolph Green or Lenny Bernstein who were also his good friends. But if their work didn't suit him, he could and did drop them or the project without stopping to change shoes. That wasn't atypical behavior; there is no director's handbook for morals. Or for success, commercial or artistic, unfortunately—that's the handbook that would really sell, more to seekers after commercial success than artistic. There are two or three firm ideas what is artistic and how to attain artistic success, but no one has a clue what is commercial and how to attain commercial success—the biggest are purely accidental. Why the vast majority of musical makers seek the commercial rather than the artistic may be because they at least know what they don't know, and anyone can win the lottery.

Jerry refused to put *Gypsy* into rehearsal until he had a box around his name. My contract called for equal billing. Stalemate. Solved by Merrick giving me an extraordinarily larger royalty—which really was paid by Leland Hayward, not Merrick. Once he had won the battle for the box, Jerry set about exercising the power now firmly in his directorial hands and Merrick set about trying to disabuse him of the belief that he had that power. If Leland Hayward had a function, it was to protect Jerry, but he wasn't around enough to do it. He and his glam wife, Slim Hawks, wafted in and out of rehearsals on their way to and from the Colony Club, and then to and from wherever the beautiful people drank their martinis dry in Philadelphia. They were good for morale, though: they adored whatever they saw when they were in the theatre.

Merrick was bad for morale, which made him feel good. His curious belief was that a producer gets the best out of author and director if he can set them at each other's throats like Rottweilers. The box-around-the-name dust-up provided him with his antagonists: Jerry and me.

Merrick's shenanigans struck me as funny. He prowled the back of the New Amsterdam roof in New York, where we rehearsed, and the back of the Shubert in Philadelphia, where we tried out, constantly muttering that the director was killing the golden goose. "Turkey lurkey!" he warned, making me laugh and making him wonder why I was laughing. He made a daily pit stop to needle me with variations on one theme: Jerry might be a great choreographer, but this was a book show; Jerry couldn't direct his way out of a paper bag and was ruining my show.

He himself believed his dire predictions for *Gypsy*: the show had Robbins cancer, he had seen the X rays, the odds were against survival. Because Merman's last show, *Happy Hunting,* had been a flop, there was no life at the box office in New York, only a minimal advance, which the discouraging word heard from Philadelphia hadn't increased. Unless we got really good reviews, he confided, we'd close in three weeks. And considering the mess Jerry was making, close in three weeks he was certain we would.

"If you really believe that," I goaded, "why don't you sell your share to Leland and get out?"

He mulled that over for less than two seconds, then smiled. He was agreeable. Leland was more than agreeable. The deal was made, but a deal with David Merrick was a David Merrick deal, which meant it was open ended.

Opening night in New York, it was he, not Leland, who came over to my table at Sardi's, holding out the *New York Herald Tribune* review with Walter Kerr's famous opening line, "The best damn musical I've seen in years!" "This is for you," he smiled, happier than I'd ever seen him. But the review was for *his* show. He had waited and had never signed the deal. In every sense, *Gypsy* was a David Merrick production.

Leland took it with grace and good humor. At heart, he wasn't really a producer. He married famous, classy ladies and he had his table at the very classy Colony, but his business was his roster of famous, classy clients. Basically, Leland Hayward was an agent. David Merrick was a producer. His life was producing; he loved producing, he loved theatre. Today, there is a desperate need for producers who really love theatre as theatre, not for what it can do for them and their investors. David Merrick, of the slippery reputation and the slipping toupee, really loved theatre. He understood that there were two basic kinds and he produced each under a different rubric: the commercial *Hello, Dolly!* was produced by David Merrick; the artistic *Marat/Sade* was produced by his Foundation. What is surprising and encouraging is that his artistic ventures had a much higher percentage of success than his commercial ones. But it was the commercial successes that made the big money that enabled him to take risks, and he was always ready to take them.

That was why I persuaded Steve Sondheim that we bring our unconventional *Anyone Can Whistle* to Merrick. David was hardly blind to what the show was. He wasn't afraid of it or of me directing as well as writing (anathema to producers, ignoring the history of the theatre), but he believed it called for unconventional producing. A smaller theatre—the Royale, as the Bernard B. Jacobs was called then, rather than the usual big musical house like the

Majestic (where it ended up, literally)—and a smaller orchestra, sixteen rather than the usual twenty-odd. That was for starters. His objective was to lower production and running costs so that he would have extra money to promote the show after the mixed reviews he was certain it would get. To me, as director more than as author, this made eminent sense. To Steve, this was just an everyday household word I am still waiting to appear in the *New York Times*: bullshit. He believed Merrick didn't like his score and didn't want to give him the full orchestra he wanted. So the authors rejected Merrick: "You can't fire us, we quit," as Steve saw it. I like to think *Whistle* would have been different if David had produced it. And it would have been—if only because we wouldn't have had to do the thirty-two auditions we needed to raise the money for the Kermit Bloomgarden production. Kermit had no power; I had no power; the show had no power. The result was inevitable, but we were blind to that. It's common to be blind to the obvious traps that lie ahead for musicals.

Ideally, a director should know what and what not to expect from the producer before the contract is signed. After all, they know each other's résumé, they discuss the script and the score, they talk. The director and the authors talk. The director and the actors talk. *Everyone* talks—but before the first week of rehearsal is over, all parties realize they haven't been speaking the same language.

Ideally, the producer functions as the eyes and ears that can point out to the director and the authors the difference between their intentions and what is on the stage. In practice, everyone needs glasses and no one quite understands exactly what anyone else's intention was or is.

Ideally, everyone should be striving for the same goal. With *West Side Story*, we were, a major reason why the show succeeded. Power was never an issue. After its success, the ego-power shit hit the fan, but that didn't matter in the long view. The goal had been achieved, the work was completed; the triumph resulting is in evidence to this day. The active producers, Hal Prince and Bobby Griffith, joined the first producer, the loyal Roger Stevens, in time to provide enough power to balance Jerry's.

For the first-time director of a musical, the power is hardly in contest. The producer has done the hiring, the producer is taking the risk; the power is in his hands. As a result, throughout rehearsals, the director is looking over his shoulder for his replacement lurking in the shadows. Not an inspiriting way to work, assuredly not if you're working for a producer like David Merrick, and my first time out as director of a musical was working for him on *I Can Get It for You Wholesale,* a curious choice for each of us. It was adapted by Jerome Weidman from his best-selling novel and upped with music and lyrics by Harold Rome. The material wasn't particularly fresh: its central character, Harry Bogen, was an antihero, unusual perhaps for a musical but familiar because he was a smaller, paler, less theatrical Sammy Glick. Weidman's setting was not glittering Hollywood but the garment industry—and not the colorful side, as in *The Pajama Game,* that birthed tune-bright songs and dances, but the drab side known as the rag trade, which in *Wholesale* inspired songs like "Ballad of the Garment Trade," to be sung (according to the stage direction) by the company marching down Seventh Avenue (how did Harold Rome imagine that would be staged?); "Eat a Little Something," a plea by Harry's not unexpectedly Jewish kvetch of a mother; and a climactic dirge for his bankrupt clothing company: "What Are They Doing to Us Now?" Merrick had made his theatre name (and a good deal of money) with Harold Rome's musical *Fanny* (the word "musical" may seem gratuitous, but read the sentence without it), which explains to some extent why he wanted to produce *Wholesale.* Why he wanted me to direct it, I had to assume, was because he couldn't get anyone better. Or perhaps, to be a little kinder to myself, because he knew *Wholesale* needed a director unafraid of gritty material, and what was grittier than *West Side Story? Gypsy?*

But why did I want to direct something so flawed, so unmarked for success? The question was asked by Tom Hatcher, the first theatre question he asked me. We had been together five years, but in the beginning he had been an actor. Deciding he wasn't good enough, he became a contractor—why and how is for another place—which led to real estate in Quogue: an easier progression to follow, but details are also for another place. Success there led to the security to ask that first question; in our fifty-two shared years, he asked a great many more. Each, like the first, was precisely the right one to ask and was asked when and how it was best for me. I trusted him, I respected him, and soon, I depended on him. Every director needs someone to ask those questions, but not someone whose job depends on him, who reveres him blindly or is afraid to challenge him or isn't as smart as he is. Fortunately, I had Tom. I still hear his voice.

My answer to his first question was the undecorated truth, because I was secure with him: I wanted to direct *Wholesale* because I wanted to direct a musical and David Merrick had asked me. Secondly, and I admitted it was second, because I believed I could make something out of the piece, however flawed. Tom raised an eyebrow but said nothing. I may have encouraged myself to believe what I could accomplish—it's often necessary to do that, and it helps—but I really did believe I could bring *Wholesale* home.

Uncharacteristically, Merrick didn't flaunt his power. The budget was small, but that didn't faze me. I knew the show needed imagination more than money. A limited amount of the latter forces an almost unlimited supply of the former. He let me have the cast and designers I wanted. He gave me complete freedom at rehearsal.

I Can Get It for You Wholesale's strength—if it had one, and if it didn't, what it did have that could be made into a strength—was a tough, cynical attitude toward society. Harold Rome was a political being; his score emphasized that side. To me, *Wholesale* had the advantage of not being an ordinary Broadway musical. I wasn't unaware that it was not a desirable Broadway musical, either, except that it had a sarcastic energy, a drive, a reality almost exotic for musicals that gave it a touch of importance—or could have were it better written, and if the authors had the musical in their bones. Harold Rome, for all his experience, didn't any more than Weidman did. My task was to bring the show to theatrical life and make it seem as good as they thought it was.

There were three ways to accomplish that: by the look of the show, by the attack on the musical numbers, and—odd though it seemed then—by the acting. The acting most of all. The development of musical theatre and the diminishment of star power and musical prowess were giving acting an importance equal to singing and dancing. Not that it often lives up to that ranking now, nor that it's easy to do. The contrary, really. Few musically trained performers are comparably or even fairly well-trained actors. Moreover, acting in a musical is different from acting in a play. It has to be heightened; the actors have to be larger than life in order to make the transition fluid from speaking to singing or from walking to dancing. Consciously or unconsciously, experienced musical performers know this; ironically, it may make them *too* larger than life even for a musical. At the first note of the rehearsal piano, out comes the equivalent of that invisible cloak tossed around by their counterparts playing Shakespeare and out the window goes believability. What must come first, what is basic to acting in a musical, is grounding the performance in emotional reality. That, of course, is basic to acting in a play, to acting in *anything*; but in a musical, that reality is harder to find and even harder to hold on to, because it is so covered with the language of the musical. The director's first task—and it's worth all the time it may take—is to make sure every one of his actors locates his emotional reality.

Good directors argue whether casting is 50 percent of direction or 60 percent, but for all directors, good and not so, the first line to cast is for a star. The part of Harry Bogen in *Wholesale* was a starring role, but no one—not David Merrick, not his staff, not an agent in town, not I, not even the authors—believed we would get a star to play it. Harry was an antihero; antiheroes tend to be unpleasant rather than loveable, and a musical star wants to be loved. He might settle for being liked if he can still be accepted as a leading man. After fifty, he conceivably might consider playing an antihero because it could make him seem younger—forty, hopefully. Harry, however, *was* young as well as unpleasant. Thus, no one looked for a star in our firmament.

Then one turned up: the young, very popular singer Steve Lawrence. He didn't care if Harry was unpleasant; it was a juicy part, and he was so eager to get on stage, he volunteered to audition. His wife, Eydie Gormé, as good a singer and as popular a performer, came along to read with him to give him confidence. Neither had ever acted, but both had charisma which gave them a strong stage presence. Both were clearly very nice—making him wrong for Harry but making her right for Ruthie, the girl who wanted Harry. I offered her the part, but she was too much like the role: it was her fella she wanted—she wouldn't work without him.

The theatre-party vendors assured Merrick Steve Lawrence would sell, even better with Eydie Gormé. Merrick left the decision to me, proving he knew the cons as well as the pros. Steve Lawrence was so very nice and so eager, it was hard for me to say no, but I knew the show didn't stand a chance with him as Harry, pace theatre parties. The only chance it did have to succeed commercially was for it to succeed artistically. To achieve that, it had to be even tougher and funnier (which would make it tougher) than it was—and to be more a musical than it was in fact. Technically, the presence of songs made *Wholesale* a musical, but it wasn't in its bones. This wasn't being semantic; *I Can Get It for You Wholesale* was only nominally a musical. Basically, it was a dramatization of a novel with interpolated songs.

Is there a theatre form more difficult to create than the original musical? Apparently not, judging by the rarity of good originals; and most of those aren't all that original. *Urinetown, Spamalot,* and *The Drowsy Chaperone* are all examples of the trend to pastiche and, to some degree, all are in debt to *Forbidden Broadway* for teaching how to profit from the use of old musicals. Equally rare are good new musicals derived from a source, any source: plays, films, novels, short stories, biographies, pieces of journalism. "Desperate people do desperate things," Rose says in *Gypsy*; there isn't a conceivable source that hasn't been tapped. But to what end? In the beginning, even before the word, there was the question: why is it a musical?

Examine the components and begin with the beginnings of the story, because the book is where it all begins if the ambition is musical theatre. There are musicals, and successful ones, that began with a collection of songs aimed at being musical theatre. *The Boy from Oz* and *Jersey Boys* are two; both hit their primary target: the box office. The former told an interesting story badly, but it had Hugh Jackman, an exceptionally talented new musical star; the latter told a familiar story with verve and energy. The result: more entertainment for Broadway. It's music, however—songs that come from characters who come from the story—that is the making of good musicals, assuming the authors have found the right story to tell. That assumption brings up another question: what makes a story the right story for a musical? Subject matter? Setting? Characters? What?

Begin with a dry news report: a cave explorer is trapped and unable to move in a Kentucky cave. That doesn't immediately bring visions of rehearsal pianos and leg warmers, but it became *Floyd*

Collins. Begin with a somewhat legendary but unsuccessful nine-teenth-century play about pubescent sexual angst in a stifling, repressive society. That doesn't even hum and jig, let alone sing and dance, not even with the pubescent agonizers aged up to late adolescents. Nevertheless, *Spring Awakening* became better known and successful as a musical-theatre piece. What made these unlikely subjects musicals? Their creators' response to the source material. They heard song and saw musical movement where it seemingly wasn't. In both shows, the musical response had to triumph over flawed books, but triumph it did.

With *Floyd Collins,* the suspense inherent in the central situation was vitiated by the equally inherent lack of physical action; the stasis inherent in the story was countered by what tended to be more padding than invention. What made the piece a triumph of musical theatre was Adam Guettel's dazzling score, especially an innovative, mesmerizing vocal line. With *Spring Awakening,* again the heartbeat was the musical element. I'm hardly drawn to rock, but Duncan Sheik's throbbing yet lyrical score was a knockout, lifted sky high by Bill T. Jones's totally original, charged musical staging. Together with dynamic lighting and well-directed performances by the young leads, they overcame shallow lyrics and repetitious scenes in a story that is old hat today.

All credit to the creators, however: any subject matter can conceivably make not just a successful musical but exhilarating musical theatre.

A digression, but not entirely irrelevant. The standard ingredients for supposedly surefire musical theatre are larger-than-life characters, a story brimming with opportunities for theatricality, some humor, and an answer to the first question a director must ask about any theatre piece: what is it about? A paradigm source: *The Skin of Our Teeth.* Every requisite on the list and ten more. No wonder it's been made into a musical only God (and the Thornton Wilder estate) knows how many times. Nevertheless, it has never worked as a musical. Why not? Because it already *is* a musical; it just doesn't have music.

A proviso to the assertion that any subject matter can make a musical: no one asks why the characters are singing. But if no one does, why don't they? Nine times out of ten, not because of the characters, but because of the style in which their words and music are written and the setting for the story.

Choose an unlikely subject to sing about: the weather. No storms: too dramatic. A humid summer night, then; outdoors in a crowded city. The song? "Too Darn Hot," from Cole Porter's *Kiss Me, Kate.* Sung by whom where? A couple of tap dancers in the alley outside a stage door where sculpted bodies loll on fire escapes and hatch covers, fanning sexy faces and gymnasiumed torsos, and mopping unlined brows before their owners join the tapsters and begin dancing feverishly in the humidity. The choreography gets increasingly energetic and acrobatic to chorus after chorus after chorus until the chorus is pouring sweat. Why the endless dancing if it really is too darn hot? Because the number appears natural in the greasepaint style of this revival, and the exhausted audience gives it a big hand.

Years earlier, another song on the same unlikely subject was sung by very different characters in a very different style of words and music in a very different setting: a New York City tenement. The source was *Street Scene,* the naturalistic Pulitzer Prize play by Elmer Rice. Chunks of the original dialogue were kept by Kurt Weill and Langston Hughes, who found its musical equivalent in their first song: "Ain't It Awful, the Heat?," sung by blue collars hanging out the tenement windows and slumping on the stoop in front. The people, the music, the idiomatic words, all perspired. Singing seemed completely natural.

The one time out of ten when the characters themselves are the reason singing seems natural, it's because of what they are as characters. Much larger than life outside, but it's what's inside that produces the music. Sweeney Todd is frighteningly still outside, Rose is cheerfully threatening outside; inside, both are frustrated fury. His emerges icily, then builds angrily until it erupts into an almost operatic volcano of hatred and vengeful determination; hers starts with a brassy, jokey drive, then builds angrily until it shatters in a jazzed-up rage of hatred and wrenching determination.

The characters themselves can also be why they don't sing— or shouldn't sing. Henry Higgins in *My Fair Lady* has several what are called songs, but he doesn't sing them; he talks them rhythmically—not because Rex Harrison, who created the role, couldn't sing, but because Henry Higgins was too buttoned up, too much the pedant, too emotionally repressed to sing. Then he falls in love. Then and only then, for the first time in his hitherto dried leaf of a life, Henry Higgins sings, Rex Harrison sings, a haunting love song: "I've Grown Accustomed to Her Face." (Also sung by Marlene Dietrich in her cabaret act, without a change of pronoun and with equal effect. Love levels.)

Sometimes a character sings before he should. This was the case in *Do I Hear A Waltz?* by Richard Rodgers and Stephen Sondheim and me. The character was not a he but a she—the heroine, Leona Samish. Leona had come to Venice to find love but was too wary, too suspicious, too emotionally throttled. She herself says that when she falls in love, she'll hear a waltz—i.e., music. That, then, is when she should have sung, but she was trilling away long before that. I should have known it was a mistake: the musical was adapted from my play *The Time of the Cuckoo* (later disguised as a movie travelogue called *Summertime*), and no one knew Leona better than I. But I was too eager to get the show on and checked my musical brains. Singing too early muddied the character and weakened the show.

Ideally, a song in a musical-theatre piece should be a one-act play with a beginning, middle, and end. Such a song moves the play forward and almost stages itself for the director. Unfortunately, most songs in musical theatre are still songs of musical comedy: the lyric states one thought, repeats it over and over, and ends with a slight verbal twist. Essentially, nothing happens emotionally and the song goes nowhere, forcing the director into staging that is static or the choreographer into whipping up compensatory frenetic dances from nowhere. Most of the songs in *I Can Get It for You Wholesale* were of that nature, but I had a cast that included two beginners who became stars, Barbra Streisand and Elliott Gould (who played Harry), and two former stars, Lillian Roth and Harold Lang. Most of the others were exceptional dancers, a few were exceptional singers, and all could act. With that company, the prosaic flatness of *Wholesale* and its songs could be given theatrical life. The director could use his imagination, trusting his players to make his inventions work. They made mine even seem inspired.

Example: "Ballad of the Garment Trade," scripted to be sung marching down Seventh Avenue. Because the settings were so ordinary and untheatrical, I had the whole show designed in stark black, white, and gray with an arbitrary slash of color for each scene: morning blue for the kitchen, lipstick red for the nightclub, tarnished gold for the office, etc. There was a modestly stunning backdrop of the city that suggested Seventh Avenue. The company could have marched east and west, north and south in front of it to the martial rhythm of the song, singing its litany of the risks of being in the dress business—a presumably comedic litany: "If you're not [a success], you haven't got a pot to sew with." Even if I had thought the lyric could be depended on, it didn't get anywhere, and the marching wouldn't, either. So I had the song sung by various workers in the dress house Harry had taken over (by cutting corners and throats) as they built his new showroom-with-a-stage for a rag-trade fashion show that climaxed the number and the act.

This set up the climactic number in the second act, "What Are They Doing to Us Now?," sung by the employees (led by a magnetically intense Barbra Streisand despite incongruous Anna May Wong fingernails) as the pieces of the showroom and the furniture were literally taken out from under them. What made it especially effective was that by the time the plaintive number came around, the audience knew each of the people involved as a character and what the loss of the business meant to each of them. That was because each actor had gone beyond the printed page and created a person.

"Eat a Little Something" had another lyric that repeated one thought, went nowhere, and thus presented a staging problem. In the script, Harry's mother (Lillian Roth) sang the song; then Harry confessed to her that he had betrayed his partner, stolen his money, and destroyed the business. Intercutting the song and the monologue made a moving one-act play.

I Can Get It for You Wholesale began its out-of-town tryouts in Philadelphia. *I Can Get It for You Wholesale* bombed in Philadelphia. It bombed badly: the reviews even said it was anti-Semitic.

With the authority of experience, I can say that in that situation, it's worse to be the director than the author. Much worse in a musical, because there are more people—more authors, more producers, more actors, more crew, more world—who look desperately to the director to have the answer, to make it all nice and jovial and a hit. Before directing my first musical, I had decided that unlike other directors, I would put the authors first and respect their work. Rome, Weidman, and I had worked like a pothead ménage à trois during rehearsals. They brought me presents (cashmere!); they wanted me, rather than Herb Ross, the choreographer, to stage the songs. Then Philadelphia and bombs away. Now whose side was I on?

It's right and it's necessary to respect the authors' work. But for a director to position himself "on their side" is asking for trouble and ignoring that there can be only one side for a director: the show's side. Not even his own side—meaning how he has directed the piece or executed his conception (assuming he has one, and these days he would be drummed out of the corps if he didn't). Nor can he be on the star's side, should there be a star; for while it's true that if the star doesn't work, the show doesn't work, the star has to work *for* the show. I remember a meal at Sardi's with Barbara Harris—one of the most sublime musical actors I have ever seen—after a preview of *The Apple Tree.* She brushed aside my praise (she couldn't accept compliments anyway) to ask a question that answered itself: "But the show doesn't work, does it?" She knew; she had asked it before and had known the answer about *On a Clear Day.* The show is what matters, the show the audience sees on the stage, not the show so many involved think they see. The director has to see and hear what the audience is seeing and hearing, particularly when what is being seen and heard is not working; and alas, alack, and lackaday, what was on that stage in Philadelphia was not working. When that happens, everyone involved, top to bottom, turns to the director.

Whether they turn with hope and confidence or with fear and desperation depends not only on the director's record and reputation but on the face he wears when he comes to the first meeting after those reviews that have struck terror. Terror can engender panic, insanity—at the least, clinical depression. Usually, the tension is relieved by firing the costume designer, but *Wholesale's* designer wasn't important enough to be fired (the legendary Theoni Aldredge in her first Broadway musical), and anyway, Merrick wasn't about to spend money on a replacement.

He came to the panic production meeting in a surprisingly

jovial mood. He was anticipating the Rottweilers would be un-leashed. I disappointed him. I was calm and genial (fear success-fully hidden) and laid out what I thought had to be done. Jerry and Harold agreed, went off to work, and I went off to face the company.

The trick, in those sessions, is for the director, when he speaks, to look intently just to the right of the eyes of someone in the fifth row; then, at intervals, to shift to someone farther back and to one side, then to the other side—always careful to look at a forehead, never, never in anyone's eyes. What the Father of Us All is doing is trying to convince, not a band of frightened players, but a bunch of skeptical actors who nevertheless are eager to be convinced of what he's trying to convince himself: that the problem with the show is easy to fix. When Oscar Hammerstein and Richard Rodgers came to accursed Philadelphia to see what *Gypsy*'s prob-lem was, they said: Fix the doorknob on the dressing-room door in the last scene and that will do it. Literally, that's what they said. Well, that was *Gypsy*, and they weren't right anyway.

Wholesale had one problem the cast knew. How they knew was a mystery, but they always know, and how is always a mystery. They knew the producer wanted to fire Elliott Gould, the leading man, and Barbra Streisand, who was stealing the show, or would have been had there been a show to steal. Merrick thought both were too homely. They couldn't have disagreed more; they were falling in love. Merrick went after me like a dog after a bone to fire them; he was relentless—he wouldn't quit until he got that bone. He was all smiles, but it was undeclared war.

Even in Boston, where the rewritten show was a hit, he kept after me, concentrating on Elliott, who was drenching the first rows with sweat when he danced. We called Dr. "Miracle" Max Jacobson in New York; he prescribed a pill that stopped the sweat-ing but dried up Elliott's vocal cords so he couldn't sing. Merrick flew in replacements from Hollywood. One of them was Michael Callan, who as Mickey Calin had been the original Riff in *West*

Side Story: very magnetic, and he danced without watering the first rows. When I finally said "Enough!" and told Merrick to stop wasting his money on plane fare because I was not going to fire Elliott, Nora Kaye (who was assisting her husband, Herb Ross, with the choreography) burst into tears—not because of any principle upheld but because she believed in Elliott's talent. Dancers, like other minorities, stick together.

Some months after the show opened in New York, Merrick brought in another *West Side* alumnus, Larry Kert, who did replace Elliott. By that time, Elliott and Barbra were living happily together in Harry Hart's red West End Avenue apartment and their eyes on the next yellow brick road.

When a show is in trouble, out of town or in, the director has got to move and to move fast in behalf of every name on the billboard, which put together don't spell mother but the whole show. The terror-prompted rewrites Jerome Weidman handed me in Philadelphia were bewildering, even embarrassing.

"If I give these to the cast, they'll laugh," I told him.

"I meant them to laugh," he said, laughing himself. Jerome Weidman meant for the actors to laugh at his rewrites? Fear, bluster, but he said that sentence quote unquote.

There was my resolve to respect the authors and there was Weidman's sentence, which kept reverberating. I thought more rewriting was needed; he didn't—or he didn't think he could do more. And I didn't disagree with him: I dropped my resolve and picked up the yellow legal pad and the Blackwing pencil.

The charge of anti-Semitism, I ignored. The protagonist of *I Can Get It for You Wholesale,* the antihero played by Elliott Gould, is a Sammy Glick cousin in the garment industry. There will always be those who say such a character is anti-Semitic; their number will depend on how successful the show is. The actual impediment to *Wholesale's* success came largely from fidelity to its source: the novel. Novels are better adapted to the screen. Generally loosely structured, their ruminative qualities are unsuited to musical theatre, where economy and bold strokes are a necessity. They are what give a show pace and drive; walking in the footprints of a novel throws off the rhythm, both in individual scenes and in the show as a whole.

Cutting and editing Weidman's script to clean out dross and get pace came easily. Rewriting dialogue to replace statements of theme with brief, pointed emotional outbursts brought qualms but wasn't hard. Restructuring to bring kinetic energy to the scene-song predictability, to syncopate its rhythm theatrically, wasn't so easy, but I knew where to dive in. I hadn't done so before because of my determination to respect the text. Respect shouldn't come with the territory; it should be merited.

Just before we left Boston, I made a mistake I've never forgotten. I've never made it again.

The last scene in the play, a coda really, was a brief meeting between a down-and-out Harry and Ruthie, the girlfriend he had jilted. She still wants him; he's not interested in her until she mentions she's inherited a little money. Back to life comes Harry with a wild-eyed grin that makes the audience laugh even as it shudders.

I staged the scene in front of the drop that suggested Seventh Avenue. Racks of dresses were pushed across the stage from both sides, criss-crossing each other to music. One crossing rack revealed Harry; another, from the opposite direction, revealed Ruthie. They smile, she wistfully, he politely; they make talk, and she mentions her inheritance. Everything is suddenly suspended in mid silent air. The music stops; the audience watches and waits. Then Harry grins and the orchestra plays "The Sound of Money," a song Harry had sung earlier. An effective ending: applause started even as the curtain started down.

Then I had a last-minute idea I thought rang the bell figuratively as well as literally. It went in at the last Wednesday matinee in Boston. When the inheritance was mentioned and everything and everyone was suspended in a breathless pause, the silence was broken by the ping of a cash register. That was what made Harry grin, cueing "The Sound of Money."

I loved it. The audience didn't. The ping shocked it into a unanimous, audible gasp of revulsion. When the curtain started down, there was no applause.

That it was a Wednesday-matinee audience of Boston ladies, that the shock and the gasp were really the reaction I wanted, I ignored. I ran scared. I cut the cash register and didn't even think of trying it again at a preview in New York.

Nothing in the show made the point of the story as economically, as theatrically, as well overall as the sound of that cash register. It was the kind of moment you remember long after you've seen the show. It might have helped *Wholesale* immeasurably. It might also have merely been a moment that came and went. But I cut it because the audience response had made me afraid the cash register was too much, too obvious, over the top, too naked a statement. In my gut it was right for the show and a directorial touch to be proud of, but I cut it because one audience had made me afraid.

When I returned to this country after living in Paris because I'd been blacklisted here during the Hollywood Witch Hunt, I wouldn't sign petitions or give my name or money to anything. It hadn't been easy to get my passport back, and quite simply, I was afraid. I can claim I was being practical, and in time the fear did evaporate. Pair that with one moment in a musical? One cut made because of one audience's reaction, one betrayal of oneself? Yes; the thwarted principle behind each was the same: do what you believe.

One misstep can set a pattern—in the theatre, particularly if the show concerned does well. *Wholesale* did very well for me, but my misstep set no pattern. It was a mistake, and when the air cleared, I wasn't easy on myself for making it.

After Tom died, my values got clearer and firmer. I wasn't going to do anything in the theatre unless it really excited me, and then I would do it the way I believed it should be done or not at all. That was tested several times during *Gypsy*; one provided a special lesson. A man I respected and whose opinion meant a great deal to me saw a preview at the St. James and called me the next day to tear the show to shreds. There wasn't a positive anything when he finished. I had overdone everything; Patti was terrible, angry from start to finish; "Rose's Turn" was totally incomprehensible and a mess; Laura's laughter when she walked off at the end was the cruelest thing he'd ever seen in the theatre. He followed up with a two-page e-mail that was vicious with details. The unexpectedness of the attack had shock value. I said nothing; I didn't answer his e-mail (but I printed it out as a reminder).

Because it was he, I was shaken. For a long moment. Then I heard him saying Patti's Rose was angry from start to finish. That, I could truly be objective about. Patti LuPone's Rose was more fun and funnier, sexier, more loving even in the early scenes than any Rose he or anyone else ever saw. He was wrong—dead, fabricated wrong. Clearly his opinion didn't come from a performance he saw on the stage of the St. James but from something askew inside him.

I never mentioned to him the phenomenal response of the audience every night, including the night he saw it. Nor did I mention later the phenomenal, unanimous response of the press. I didn't expect him to, either, and he didn't; but he had to know about it—he read the *Times*. Both audience and press were welcome validation.

And necessary.

No, you say?

Yes, I say. I remember the attack because I respected the attacker, just as I remember the praise because of my respect and admiration for the man it came from. But I would have done what I did without a word one way or the other from either of them or anyone else. That's what I learned from him.

Moral: do what you believe in.

(Laughing): Can't we put it another way that doesn't sound so much like a candidate for a needlepoint pillow? Never do what you don't believe in. Even if it's successful, it isn't worth it.

Really?

Really. Not for me. You won't keep me in my seat for your second act just because you're a hit. I won't expect you to stay in your seat for mine unless it's theatre as you dreamed it would be, or why am I doing it?

FIVE

Smoke and Mirrors

S INCE IT'S ALWAYS BEEN NEXT to impossible to find a happy
homosexual on the Broadway stage who is still happy at the
final curtain, the notion of a multimillion-dollar Broadway musical with *two* happy homosexuals on stage at the final curtain
seemed completely impossible to me. That it would be adapted
from a successful movie didn't make it any less so.

The movie was a little French farce called *La Cage aux Folles.* Its
success in this country was surprising, for its hero was a drag
queen. In France, drag is a tradition; in the United States, drag is a
camp or a sin, frequently both. In Hollywood, there was a producer for whom camp, as much as box-office success, made the
film a hot property. His name was Allan Carr. Famous, locally anyway, for his insane parties at the old Ingrid Bergman house in Beverly Hills and then for cleaning up with *Grease,* Carr was serious
about *Cage* for Broadway. He took off his caftan, put on a blue
blazer, and came east to turn a camp French film into a camp
musical, innocently certain he had a smash hit on his hands. He
wanted me to direct.

I didn't want to direct: drag turned me off. In life, I was introduced to it at my first meeting of the Gay Activists Alliance at
the old Firehouse in the Village. Tom Hatcher had joined the Alliance much earlier and brought me into the fold. When I walked
through the Firehouse door, I felt I was politically home again.
The battered jeans, the scraggly beards, the "Point of order! Point

of order!"—all the appurtenances of the left-wing past I had been missing were there. The desired effect of the Hollywood Witch Hunt had been silence. Now that silence was broken, and by more than the usual voices overshouting each other. This was a kind of screeching from fiery protesters with wild mops of hair in embroidered tunics worn over battered jeans and muddy work boots: drag queens of the gay revolution—aka transvestites ranting against "straight" gays who, they claimed, were ashamed of them and trying to push them out of the Gay Liberation picture. They were right; they still are.

Drag in the theatre wasn't to my taste, either. I didn't and don't consider all-male productions like Clifford Williams's *As You Like It* at the Old Vic in London in the sixties as drag. Brilliant acting added a new dimension to the play: was Orlando in love with Rosalind as a woman or as a man pretending to be a woman? Real drag I first saw in the theatre—a facsimile of theatre, really—much earlier, in Greenwich Village, where abbreviated versions of hit Broadway musicals were performed with switched-gender casts. A *Pal Joey* featured the most elegantly witty Vera I've ever seen. Played by a man dressed as a woman, Lynne Carter was technically a drag queen, but too good an actor to be slotted in any category. Still, drag it was.

The unforgettable Charles Ludlam, who had his own theatre on Sheridan Square, was also an actor and also a drag queen. His drag in *Camille* was ridiculous, as was everything he wore and did, most spectacularly his classic *Mystery of Irma Vep* with Everett Quinton. I never saw as much of Ludlam and his Ridiculous Theatrical Company as perhaps I should have; the drag on stage inevitably became tiresome to me because of the exaggerated costumes and the camp humor that came with it mercilessly. A limitation on my part? I also think certain Samuel Beckett plays are the Emperor's New Clothes.

I don't dismiss out of hand. I always went, I always saw. Years ago, when the theatre was awash in New Theatre, I got Richard Poirier to go with me to a Richard Foreman Ontological-Hysteric Theatre play. As customary, the stage was sectioned with lines of string, and light bulbs wavered at random. When the play was over, the author of *The Performing Self* was succinct: "A crock," he said. Does that validate my opinion? Does the wholesale acclaim of the upper intellectual strata validate every stage direction by Beckett? Time validates, but how much, and for how long? The avant garde does influence now and then, but everything changes except the avant garde. Eventually, praise be, theatre returns to character and story. Ideas come naturally and so, happily, can passion, scorned though it is at the antiseptic moment.

I'm still open to the new; I go, though not as often as before. I want to leave a theatre glad I came; now it's an effort not to leave at the intermission. Nor am I alone. There is a distinct trend to intermissionless works. Once in a while there's water in the Sahara: *Spring Awakening*. I admired and enjoyed it. The reviewers went overboard. The work would forever alter musical theatre, they announced. So did the authors. It won't. Does that matter? If the creators of the show believe it, yes; if the readers believe it, yes, because the next time they read it, they will cry wolf. What I think will have a lasting influence in *Spring Awakening* is the musical staging. It's truly an innovation in staging musical numbers. There have been changes in doing such: the snaking microphones across faces, including those of lovers trying to kiss, in *Rent*; the handheld phallic microphones the boys whip out in *Spring Awakening* as though they were whipping out their penises, which is what they are meant to look like—but not in *Jersey Boys,* where a handheld microphone is a handheld microphone. All the flaunted microphones have been influences that I doubt will last—they're too limiting. There's also John Doyle's use of instruments: very effective in a humorous *Sweeney Todd,* annoying in a manufactured *Company* (which was in desperate need of a choreographer), a gimmick if used again. The musical staging in *Spring Awakening,* however, is direct from the characters, the story, the milieu, the passions, and thus points where to go and what to do when you get there: *think, imagine, create.*

I agreed to direct *Cage* because I thought the production would never happen. Allan Carr had come a cropper trying to produce it, his first Broadway adventure, with a Vegas touch. The *Cage aux Folles* set on the French Riviera in the movie was to become *The Queen of Basin Street,* set in New Orleans, for the musical, with direction by Mike Nichols, choreography by Tommy Tune, score by Maury Yeston, and book by Jay Presson Allen (who began with the stage direction "The décor is early faggot," and that's as far as I read). The combined royalties of these boldface names guaranteed financial failure for producer and investors, as Fritz Holt and Barry Brown told Carr, who promptly hired them as executive producers. They fired everybody. The resulting lawsuits were lost by all except Maury Yeston, who got a small royalty; and the boys—producers and creators alike are always "the boys," except when they're "the ladies"—started out afresh by approaching me.

Why me? Because Fritz and Barry's first production—and their first success—was the *Gypsy* I had directed with Angela Lansbury. It was also their only success so far. We'd had a lot of fun and become friends in the process; they were still stagestruck—and they were broke. I said yes because it would keep them on Allan's payroll until he—and they—faced the fact they would never find enough investors. Certainly not at a time when the battle between gay liberation and political homophobia was intensifying, and the longer-and-longer-running box-office queens were syrupy sung-through scenic spectacles from London.

Then Fritz told me they had signed Jerry Herman and Harvey Fierstein for the project. The Jerry Herman of *Hello, Dolly!* and *Mame* and their title songs was very right for *La Cage aux Folles*; the Harvey Fierstein of *Torch Song Trilogy* was, to me, *the* contemporary gay voice. Both were very excited that I (presumably) was

going to direct. (They loved *Gypsy*. What musical-theatre afi-
cionado didn't?)

"Wait till you see Jerry's house," Fritz said, urging a meeting.
"There's a trapeze on the top floor where you'll work!" The meeting was scheduled. Fritz was very enthusiastic. (He was always
enthusiastic, even the day he died of AIDS.) He glossed over the
fact that the boys had nothing on paper: they had "terrific ideas."
And as he was on his way out the door: "Oh, by the way, Allan
doesn't have the rights to the film, but he does have the rights to
the original play by Jean Poiret—it's a knockout!" I'm a quick
reader, and I read the play before the meeting at Jerry's. It was *not*
a knockout; the meat and potatoes of the story were in the film,
not the play. Some people buy a house without looking in the
closets.

But Jerry had written a song.

Jerry Herman had a profitable hobby: buying and decorating
houses, and selling them quickly. The studio where he played
that crucial song for Harvey and me was on the top floor of his
own Jerry Herman–decorated house in the East Sixties. He sat at a
polished grand piano with that trapeze hanging overhead. The
song was typical of the anthems sung by the heroine in all his
musicals—except that this one went much further. To be sung by a
gay man, it had balls and anger; a relevance to the times made it
political, intentionally or not. Jerry played and sang it with a passion that made me sit up. It was *his* anthem; it became ours, the
gay community's: it became the Gay Anthem. It was called "I Am
What I Am."

Jerry meant for it to end the first act, sung by Albin, the drag-
queen hero, but neither he nor Harvey knew where Albin was
singing it or why he was singing it at that particular moment.
There wasn't an outline; they hadn't really talked; they didn't have
"terrific ideas." The original play asked more questions than it
answered. They looked expectantly at me, their (presumed) direc-

tor, for answers—and judging by my reaction to the song, why not?

It had really gotten to me. I began to answer my own questions. The song had to be sung in drag; that would mean sung in the nightclub where the play took place, but not as a number, because then it would merely be a message sung by a performer, not a character; and not without a motivation, because then it would merely be a number in a show. It had to be an emotional outburst, but what did it burst out of? I was so wired by the song that in two minutes, more or less, I had answers, and the first act began to take shape. If the opening number of the Broadway show was also the opening number of the cabaret show at the Riviera nightclub, and if that number was a chorus of drag queens singing "*We* Are What We Are," it would set up both the whole show and the ending of the first act.

Very relieved, the boys beamed. Harvey had been a drag queen but had never written a musical. Jerry had written scores and contributed to books, but it was the director who usually took the material and shaped it for the show. What I had just done was what they expected me to do: take something that had been written, that anthem, and figure how to make it work. They were elated; they had their director; *La Cage aux Folles* was under way.

Was it? Was I really hooked by one song?

Perhaps because I was a playwright, one of the things that attracted me to directing musicals was the opportunity to be creative and inventive. It was constantly knocking, and I loved answering as I had just done. It was tempting to sign on (and make Fritz happy as well), but something else weighed in more heavily. That something had always been there, but I had let my distaste for drag and camp get in the way.

Two homosexuals at the center of a musical. Two gay men. Two gay men happy at the final curtain. Of a big Broadway expense-account musical. Was that possible? Reaching higher: a Broadway musical to which the unconverted came and left glad they came? Questioning the beliefs they held before they came? Was *that* possible? Could that be achieved?

Wasn't it worth a try?

Was that a question for a director?

If a director has political convictions, does he bring them into the theatre? Does he let them influence what play he chooses to direct and how he directs it? Rhetorical questions; of course he does. "I Am What I Am," *Torch Song Trilogy,* and the authors' eagerness for me to take charge tipped the scale. I took on *La Cage aux Folles* because I believed that men who put lampshades on their heads and tablecloths around their waists while their giggling wives squealed "Oh, Harry!," men who used the word "fag" casually—most straight American men, then—could nevertheless be gotten to applaud gays. They and theirs were the target audience, not the converted. If the show was any good, gays and the gay-friendly would provide audible support with laughter and applause. It was the enemy I was after. I knew I would have a good time trying to get them.

Jerry and Harvey and I were more than merely on the same go-get-them page. The collaboration was a joy from the first day in Jerry's studio to the last preview in Boston, where the show had its tryout. Each morning after a preview, the three of us would meet for breakfast. They would give me their notes and I would give them mine. Finally, no one had any notes, but Harvey had a request.

"I wish they would kiss at the end."

The two male leads danced off into the sunset at the end as I staged it. "Kiss where?"

On the lips would risk losing the audience we had worked so carefully to get, and Harvey knew that. "On the cheeks," he said.

"French men kiss on both cheeks regularly," I said.

"I hate it when they just touch," Jerry said, and we called for the check.

The first question when starting work on a show is: what is it about? The answer tells where to put the focus. Both play and movie focused on camp elements in the relationship between the two men. What effectively counterbalanced camp in the movie was the presence of the boy's natural mother. A very French woman, or at least what Lampshade Harry and his squealing wife would think a very French woman was: chic and sexy and a threat. A figure that could add a color to the musical, vary the tone, broaden the range, and shift the focus of the story to the boy and his mother. Except that ours couldn't. Unless we wanted to be sued, the woman couldn't appear in the musical, because she didn't appear in the play. Paradoxically, that limitation led me to what the musical *could* be about. The story was thin, even for a musical; moreover, it was neither inherently funny nor dramatic. What was needed was something to grab the audience and give it someone or something to root for. *La Cage aux Folles* the musical was going to be about a boy who comes to accept a *man* as his mother. There we were! The focus on family and off sex. And the story had an unexpected heart. Even a little heart would be a big help in a tale of two queens. Especially in a multimillion-dollar musical tale of two queens, one a drag queen, the other his lover.

That mother/son approach conceivably could be tracked to material buried in both the play and the film, but a literal adaptation wasn't desirable anyway. Literal adaptations start a musical off in trouble. No form is comfortable in another form, and the addition of music brings a change that demands change in attitudes. The adapters must be clear why they're attempting this work. What's *their* purpose? What's *their* viewpoint? To achieve the purpose, material from the original will be kept or discarded or embellished, and always as seen from a special viewpoint.

We took what we could from the Jean Poiret play and began cobbling a show. I structured; Harvey wrote scenes in a loose-leaf
notebook; Jerry wrote songs on his melodic baby grand. Work was
interrupted two or three times a week to raise money via auditions
held in Jerry's top-floor studio for investors perched everywhere,
even on the little balcony and under the trapeze. Allan was good at
rounding up money. My concentration was on testing the story as
we developed it and inventing what we hadn't gotten to. There are
worse ways of writing a musical, judging from the current crop.
Occasionally we could see which was the way to go. The emphasis
on the boy accepting a man as his mother got a tangible response:
checks! A new song Jerry sold at his piano: checks! (Jerry Herman
could have had a big career just singing and playing to raise
money.) But the Fritz Holt–like enthusiasm we were hoping for
remained elusive; the checks weren't that many or that big . . . until
one audition day an idea popped out without warning. I had
reached the section of my pitch explaining the show's chorus of
drag queens (named Les Cagelles, because it sounded French)
when I heard myself say:

"Two of them are actually girls, the rest are boys. The audience
will be trying to find out which is which, but they won't know
until the curtain call."

Not a bad idea, I thought, not at all—in fact, pretty good. *Very*
good, thought the putative investors—terrific, in fact. They
applauded—big-time, as Allan put it. They ceased being putative:
the big-money ball began rolling in. That I didn't have a clue how
Which-Cagelle-is-what? was going to be worked out didn't matter
to Allan. It *had* to be worked out; therefore, it *would* be worked
out—and he was right: it would be and it was. What I didn't and
couldn't foresee was that thanks to word of mouth and a good
press agent, Shirley Herz, Which-is-what? would become one of

the best sellers of the show. It had nothing to do with the story; it was just smoke and mirrors—the theatrical magic this musical *Cage aux Folles* needed.

Smoke and mirrors have always played an important role in musicals, most obviously through the scenery: the merry-go-round in *The Band Wagon,* the chandelier in *Phantom,* the helicopter in *Miss Saigon,* the projections in *Tommy,* the hanging starlight bulbs by Kevin Adams for *Spring Awakening.* Sometimes the smoke makes the audience cough and the mirrors are cracked—or, worse, smoke and mirrors are all there is to the show: *Miss Saigon* with its helicopter and its Cadillac and its black pajamas not intended for the sleep they brought. On the other, better hand, as in various Hal Prince–directed musicals, smoke and mirrors can derive from the material and reinforce it, even extend its horizons by making it visually exciting: the elevator in *Company,* the lascivious all-girl band rolling on stage in *Cabaret,* the Boris Aronson hanamichi pouring into the auditorium for *Pacific Overtures.* Smoke and mirrors can conceal or decorate or enlarge, and in guises other than scenery or costumes. The staging of scenes, of numbers, of what leads up to numbers—anything on stage can be smoke and mirrors, as I found out with *Cage.*

Take its opening. The vitally important first ten minutes of a musical are the first challenge for the director. The opening musical number of *Cage* was obvious: the Cagelles singing "We Are What We Are" in drag in the nightclub called La Cage aux Folles. But was that how the show would open—with a stageful of drag queens in full fig? Hit the audience smack in the face? Get it over with and confront the unconverted—the enemy? I didn't think so. The purpose of the first minutes of any musical is not to challenge the audience but to hook it so firmly it will stay hooked for half the first act. Then you can challenge away.

The French movie we couldn't use had a visually alluring opening: skimming over the glistening night water of the Mediterranean toward the lights of a Riviera cabaret spelling out "La Cage aux Folles." Effective: it made you want to go inside that club. Of course, that shot couldn't be duplicated in the theatre; but paradoxically, that was a blessing. The theatre, even the most kitchen-sink theatre with real running water from a tap, is illusion; if the movie opening could be simulated in theatre terms, no one could claim copyright violation. Simulated it was, and brilliantly, thanks to David Mitchell: a technical wizard, as a few scenic designers are; an artist, as a very few are; and a painter, which almost no one is.

As the orchestra played the overture (with Broadway-French touches like a Piaf accordion), the curtain rose on rose-hued buildings in perspective in a little plaza with the Riviera on the horizon. Lights glowed in windows as the buildings spun and parted to reveal the façade of a nightclub with "La Cage aux Folles" in lights. The buildings slid off, the club entrance rode downstage, and its doors opened to reveal gossamer white curtains. Then the icing on the magic cake of theatre: swirling white curtains billowed and spread out across the whole stage, with a LA CAGE sign glittering above it. Through the center of the parachute silk swept an elegant, tuxedoed Gene Barry, paradigm of the continental host, almost singing, "Mesdames et messieurs, welcome to La Cage aux Folles!" A punctuating chord from the orchestra and the audience went wild.

Was the idea *not* to prepare the unconverted for the drag queens to come? No, there was a hint: Gene Barry's wrist. He thought he was being continental as he flipped his palm in a welcoming gesture to the audience, but they knew better—particularly the men who had come only because of their wives. They were so impressed and glamorized, however, by the smoke and mirrors leading up to that wrist, they were *glad* they had come.

Gene Barry. What an unexpected journey we all take. Tom came to Boston for the last preview before we opened. It was a Friday night. He was complimentary; he appreciated all the smoke and mirrors. But fortunately for me, he wasn't fooled.

"You've done a wonderful job," he said. "You know I never thought much of this thing, so I'm really amazed at the level you've brought it up to. But—" I braced myself—"it's not what you want it to be, because Gene Barry isn't any good."

During rehearsals, everyone, myself included, had wanted to fire Gene, but we couldn't find anyone to replace him. It was extremely hard to find an American with the continental flair and the music-hall (vaudeville) style the role of Georges demanded. What made it harder was that the co-starring role of Albin (the wonderful George Hearn) was not only showier but had all the big numbers. Gene did have the vaudeville style, which is what had gotten him the part, but little else. A television series can be an unnoticed death to an actor's talents. But there had been no replacement to be found, and there still wasn't. I did what every director has to do in that fix: I worked hard and convinced myself Gene was getting better, Gene was becoming good, Gene *was* good. He *was* getting better, but he wasn't getting good.

I went into his dressing room before the Saturday matinee. He took one look at my look.

"No!" he said. "No! We're opening tonight!"

"Just listen to me."

"No! I will not be upset!"

"You'll be panned if you don't." He had moved to open the dressing-room door to kick me out but stopped. Gene was not a fool; he knew he was in trouble. "I can help you," I said.

"You haven't done much so far," he snapped.

"You go up on the feed line for every one of the few jokes George has. He's Irish. Next time, he'll punch you in the nose. I know why you do it, Gene. I understand. He has all the big numbers. But do what I say and I'll get you through tonight. Then I promise you we'll turn every one of those announcements of yours into an aria that will land like a musical number." That wasn't bullshit. I believed it, so he did. "For tonight, whenever you're on stage with George, never look anywhere except into his eyes. Only three people will know you're looking at his forehead—you, George, and me. The audience will think you're looking into his eyes, and this will become the most unusual love story in musical-theatre history."

He did it, and it actually worked. So did the transformation of his "Tonight, La Cage aux Folles presents the magnificent Zaza" and all its variations into emotional moments. The challenge to bring them off was one of those opportunities that attracted me to musicals. I had a really good time inventing with Gene, and the result was gratifying—not only in what it did for the show but in what it did for Gene and what it did for Gene and me. He loved being in *Cage*; his wife loved his being in *Cage*; and he loved me as a friend. He played New York for a year, then the California company for almost a year. A year or so later, he wanted to come back to the New York company. He was so happy rehearsing, so happy working with me again, so happy playing Georges again. And he was good! Unfortunately, he played only one night. He had a heart attack two hours after the performance. His life dwindled after that, but he'd had that triumphant night.

I might have developed those announcements into arias during rehearsal; I should have, because I knew even then that Gene didn't have the big moments he wanted and the character he deserved. Rehearsals aren't used nearly as much as they should be for experimenting. Actually, I did use *Cage* rehearsals to test how far I could and could not go with moments like a man singing a love song to another man for the first time in a big Broadway musical.

The day I showed the company Gene singing "Song on the Sand" to George, there were no accordion, no strings, no romantic backdrop and lighting; just a rehearsal piano and two actors sitting at a table. But the two were really into the scene—they weren't Gene and George, they were Georges and Albin. Gene might not have been very good at that stage, but he was never self-conscious about playing gay. That's rare, even today. At one point in the song, Albin reaches over for Georges's hand; then Georges puts his over Albin's. With the last note, Albin leans over and kisses Georges's hand. I looked around the rehearsal room: tears were being brushed away. Well, gypsies—what do you expect? But I watched the audiences during that song, *Boston* audiences: tears were being brushed away. The gypsies always know. If the love is believable to the characters, the audience might not like it or accept it, but they will believe it, no matter what the gender.

A cautionary note about intricate moving scenery in musicals. It can work, sometimes even at first try; but sooner or later, it won't. It will break down and there will be panic. That's where relations with the crew comes in. The first Boston preview of *Cage* had to be cancelled because the scenic sorcery of the opening didn't work. If the nightclub doors didn't jam as they slid on stage, then they jammed as they rode downstage. They jammed both times at rehearsal the next day. How could we have a performance? How could we *not*? The show had almost no advance; tickets weren't selling; it would be unfair to the producers to cancel another pre-view. The doors to the club would have to be cut, and as the revolving buildings slid off, the white curtains would come billow-ing down and spread across the stage under the glittering Cage marquee. Enough sorcery for anyone.

Not for the crew. They loved the show; they loved the cast, even though, like the Cagelles, it was mainly gay and they couldn't have been straighter. (In Australia, the Cagelles were straight, the crew was gay: that's life down under.) They loved Fritz Holt and they loved me. They begged for one more chance. They were sure they could make those sliding doors work. The cast begged for them to be given their chance; they were sure *their* crew could bring it off.

When a company is permeated with that kind of love—and it *is* a kind of love—conflicts disappear, work is a joy, and (no surprise) the show is immeasurably better. It has to be: love's involved. So it was with every company of *Cage* in this country, in London, in Sydney—and it began with that first company previewing in Boston. I gave the crew that one more chance. The club entrance doors slid on like butter—ecstasy!—and then jammed riding downstage. But no one panicked; the crew was prepared. They pushed the door unit downstage manually; they split the doors, they slid them off—and somehow, God knows how, without their being seen! They were determined it would work, and so it did. It was like being unable to get pregnant and then succeeding only after a baby had been adopted. The next performance, the doors worked mechanically as they were supposed to, and they continued to do so happily ever after.

Triumph, joy, the air shimmering with success: the audience captured by the magic of theatre, aka smoke and mirrors. All the same, no matter how you sliced it and disguised it, *La Cage aux Folles* was still a show about drag queens who were about to make their entrance in drag singing to the audience that They Were What They Were. Furthermore, the enchantment, the magic had built up their entrance so that expectancy was higher than ever. No amount of smoke and mirrors could disguise the truth that what was coming on stage was drag. And it would have been seen as such if not for the brilliance of the greatest American costume designer of her time: Theoni V. Aldredge.

There is truth and there is theatre truth. Waiting in the wings of the Colonial Theatre in Boston were men in women's robes: drag. That was the truth. What appeared on stage, however, because of the fantasy design of the robes, weren't men or boys or women or girls. What were they, then? Nothing identifiable. The theatre truth was that they were elegance of an ambiguous gender. One by one, to an insinuating vamp, these creatures glided on slowly, each with his/her back to the audience, turning when he/she reached his/her position to show an alluring face that had to be female even though the audience knew—from all the public-ity, they had to know—it was otherwise. Maybe not, though; after all, two were known to be women. When all were in place, humor came into play and tipped the scale: "We Are What We Are" was sung in voices as close to basso as possible. The audience roared; they loved the boys—or those who *were* boys.

When you attempt something new or different or merely ambi-tious, don't trust in luck. There is no good luck in theatre—unless a critic's unexpected, unfathomable (even to you) rave is consid-ered luck. Polish every detail; it's all in the details, in the individual moments. Halfway measures avail you nothing: going all out is the only chance. We were home, but we didn't let go, we locked in the details—with more smoke and mirrors: one more invention, one more surprise. The Cagelles paraded like the most elegant models, but when they were ready to remove their gilded coats, they didn't merely drop them in the wings. They moved gracefully into a row of arches that had come down, struck what seemed to be a narcis-sistic pose, and when the arches flew back up, the coats flew out with them and the creatures were now in Riviera beach pajamas, which allowed them to dance—they were all marvelous dancers. A trick, but tricks like that aren't as easy as they seem. They demand painstaking care and endless rehearsal. To work, they have to flow smoothly; when they do, the audience capitulates like children at the circus—or adults at the Cirque de Soleil. More smoke and mirrors ensured enslavement: another magical costume switch allowed highly skilled tap dancing. Then one last use, the most effective of all because it led back to *character* and *story*—always, always the goal. It's so difficult to find and get right, but without that, smoke and mirrors are just smoke and mirrors, theatrical devices to blind the audience to the emptiness on stage, the holes in the story, the lack of dimension in the characters. When used for something more than diversion and entertainment, they can make musical theatre memorable—like their last use in the open-ing number of *Cage*.

In the France of *La Cage aux Folles*, the law made drag performers remove their wigs at the end of their act to prove there was
no attempt to deceive the audience, and so the Cagelles ended the
opening number by removing their wigs with a very theatrical
flourish. Nonetheless, they didn't necessarily reveal their true gender: the longest, loveliest hair that tumbled down when the wigs
were removed didn't belong to a woman but to a startlingly beautiful young man. This confused everyone, but by then, that was
just what they wanted. What could be happier than an audience at
a musical that gets what it wants? So happy, they didn't suspect the
climax of the second act was being set up: Albin, in Chanel-like
drag, pretends to be the boy's mother. From habit, he removes
his wig at the end of a song sung to the boy, his fiancée, and
her homophobic father. Mother Albin is exposed as a man; mass
hysteria—and the play was positioned to make its point. All
the parts rarely fall into place with just one stroke as they did at
that moment. Joy for everyone—the creators, the executants, and,
above all, the customers.

That theatrical sorcery continued throughout the evening. The
lovely young girl hired as the love interest wasn't much of an
actress and less of a singer. The choreographer had to be allowed to
win one battle: the girl was a lovely dancer. Unfortunately, as it
turned out, her dance was radically shortened—as it often turns
out, because musical theatre has severely diminished the audience's
interest in Pierrot and Pierrette. She had her dancer moments nevertheless: at every entrance, she came in turning like a top, ending
in a swoon into some male's arms. Why? Because on the page, her
character was the ingénue, Pierrette, barely two-dimensional. The
turning entrance gave her a quirky touch, and the swooning added
humor and sex (the only sex in the play).

If a style is established, a character can enter walking on her
hands and the audience will buy it. The style of *Cage* was established in the first scene by the slightly off-the-wall but oddly real
behavior of the two major characters and their houseboy, Jacob—

a tricky character because he's black and gay and unbridled: a combination that can be lethal if the wrong line is crossed. Succumb to the temptation of unchecked screeching, as the tasteless revival did, and Evangelicals will rejoice. The key, as always, is emotional reality. The right emotional center and the character can safely do anything. A rejected and depressed Albin walks along the Croisette in a white suit with a white Panama hat and black sunglasses, dabbing away with a large white handkerchief edged in black. (I stole the handkerchief from John Gielgud in *The Importance of Being Earnest.*) Jacob, in a white Greek toga bordered with a black frieze, holds a large black-edged white umbrella over his adored "mistress" as they move in rhythmic grief to a classical dirge. The audience found it very funny. Smoke and mirrors.

The reaction to the show continually astonished us. Previews began in Boston in a torrid July. (*West Side Story* had begun previews in Washington in a steaming August. Does that advise opening in a heat wave? I think not.) The first preview had the audience on its feet, even in the upper balcony. The next morning, the line at the box office was so long, the producers threw caution and money to the only-metaphorical wind and brought coffee and doughnuts for everyone, even passersby on their way to work. The critics raved; the chief Boston critic made the show his personal baby and offered suggestions he expected to be taken—a dicey position I'm not sure I quite wriggled out of as we made needed changes on our own. Equally astonishing was the reaction of Garson Kanin and Ruth Gordon. The distinguished couple announced that except for *My Fair Lady*, *La Cage aux Folles* was the best musical they had ever seen in their lives. I thought they had lost their minds.

The Kanins saw the play several times. Then Garson did something that was fairly common back then but is almost unheard of today. We weren't friends: I'd been on the council of the Dramatists Guild with him; Ruth had flirted with starring as a Holocaust survivor in a black comedy of mine called *Big Potato,* but then decided she didn't have the stamina for a role so large. I knew them, that's all; but Garson called me at my hotel with a suggestion to help the new ending I had given to a shaky new comedy quartet in the second act. The suggestion gave the button to the number something I hadn't seen it needed: reality of place—Albin had entered from his bedroom when he clearly should have come from outside the house and entered through the front door. Where was all my insistence on reality? Forgotten in trying to get as many laughs as possible out of an intrinsically not very funny number. But Gar spotting that important flaw surprised me, because reality had never been evident in his work—which shows how much you can read from someone's work, or how little. Anyway, most gratefully, I jumped at his suggestion and the number really landed.

Back then, that was what theatre people did—help one another. They went out of town, eager with anticipation for a new play or musical; help was available to friends or just peers and colleagues. Today, anyone out of town to see something on its hopeful way in brings a metaphorical prayer rug which is mentally unrolled and knelt on; forehead is then touched to the floor in prayer for the disaster that the new effort has been whispered to be—a little insurance can't hurt. Back then, people were enjoyable and generous; not today, twenty-five-plus years later. The theatre today is star-entombed, largely unadventurous, centered on being profitable entertainment. Twenty-five-plus years ago, entertainment was also a goal—television's influence was firmly entrenched—but not *the* goal; there was room for the original, the innovative, and the ambitious, politically as well as artistically. The theatre season of *La Cage aux Folles* was also the season of *Sunday in the Park with George. Sunday* won the Pulitzer Prize; *Cage* swept the Tonys. Prestige for one, box office for the other—and a bio line for both.

The artistic value of prizes, including the Nobel, has always eluded me. Their luster is tarnished by too many unworthy winners, by the politicking involved, and by the insistence that there be a winner even though the candidates are unqualified and often chosen by unknown anointers. The real value of a prize like the Tony is its purpose: boosting box-office sales, interest from the road, the foreign market, stock and amateur rights—in other words, money. Artistic value can't be claimed when in the year I'm writing this, neither *LoveMusik,* the most original and inventive musical on Broadway in years, nor its director, Hal Prince, who this late in his career showed what the future of Broadway musicals might be, was nominated for anything but oblivion. Yes, the show's splendid leading actors were nominated; yes, the show had obvious faults: for one, the audience was uncertain where it was and what was going on until twenty minutes into the play; for another, the off-putting German accents used by the German characters should only have been used when they came to America, not in their homeland. But not to acknowledge the production's equally obvious accomplishments was to fail to realize what music theatre can be when it dares. Hal Prince had a slew of Tonys to boast about in his *Playbill* bio, but I suspect just a nomination for *LoveMusik* might have meant more to him than some of his winners—understandable, but, I think, mistaking the worth of the prize. What I really don't understand are actors who boast of *nominations* for a Tony or a Drama Desk or a Lower Hemisphere Award in their bios—the same actors who wind up with: "Thanks to Marci, Dwight, Jocko, Mom and Rex, the best company ever, my dresser, Uta Hagen and Jesus."

The value of smoke and mirrors to the success of a production is on a par with their value to the success of a director's career. More than the audience is fooled: nothing can make a director a Director quicker than one highly praised concept musical. Is that what directing is—expertise with smoke and mirrors? What about the performance, the acting? Who is responsible? Who is really responsible for the smoke and mirrors? Is it the director or is it the choreographer or the designer or even the author? Who stages the songs—the director, the choreographer, or both in tandem?

That last question was rhetorical in the day of *La Cage aux Folles* because the good choreographers, the grand choreographers—Robbins, Fosse, Bennett—were directors as well. Since I was directing *Cage,* it would have been pointless to ask one of those icons to choreograph, and might well have been regarded as insulting: the egos involved were not small. Consequently, there were few Broadway-experienced choreographers to consider for *Cage*—two, to be factual. Only two! Pathetic. For the others, Broadway experience was confined to being a gypsy and a onetime assistant to a second-tier choreographer/director. As it turned out, the quality of work had nothing to do with consideration of the two candidates with résumés.

Is it because plot is a basic ingredient of theatre that it infects theatre people and makes them prone to plot and connive? More often than not, a homegrown plot takes over what should be a simple, straightforward act like acquiring a choreographer. One of the two choices (ordinarily, I thought two the most desirable number in the world, but the production side of theatre isn't romantic, it's business)—one of the two was intrigued; she liked the score and liked how I saw the numbers. But I smelled a rat. Why? I'm not sure. Something seemed to be holding her back; what, precisely, I never did find out. Rejecting the job, she said she wasn't right for the show; but that's the out we all use when we want to reject an offer diplomatically. Was co-directing what she was after? I brought it up; she denied it—but since she became a hyphenate the first chance she got, that was probably what I smelled. I wasn't disappointed; my first choice was Bob Avian, who worked closely with Michael Bennett almost from the beginning of his meteoric career all the way up to *A Chorus Line.* When we met, I liked him, I felt we were in sync (how we see what we want to see!). Jerry and I were in his living room, waiting for Bob to arrive to head upstairs to the studio and go over the score with him in detail when the phone rang: Could he bring Michael? Michael Bennett, of course; there was no other Michael those days. I didn't smell a rat, I *saw* a rat—and it was a big one.

This was the musical-theatre version of Bill Clinton's first run for president: with Hillary, her husband said, we the people were getting two for one. With Michael, Avian said, we the *Cage* people were getting two for one. I didn't want another director; neither did Jerry. We wanted Avian solo, and I said so, but that didn't end the game. Michael phoned: charming, admiring, another fan of *Gypsy.* Nevertheless, it was clearly Allan Carr who would be getting two for one and not I. Michael was offering to make *Cage* his next musical, and where Michael Bennett was ranked in the Broadway hierarchy, that was an offer that was not to be refused. But Jerry Herman and I had chutzpah: we refused.

I thought it would end there, but it didn't. Allan Carr, like every producer of a musical, went looking for a Broadway theatre for the show with the theatre owner ponying up a sizeable investment. Like every musical producer, he went to the Shuberts: they have most of the best musical houses. The Shuberts were Gerald Schoenfeld and Bernard Jacobs. Today only Gerry is left; Bernie is only a theatre. (Gerry is also a theatre; the Shuberts own them both.) Gerry was more than willing to give Allan a major Shubert house plus an investment of $500,000. He had only one requirement: replace Arthur Laurents with Michael Bennett.

Gerry and Bernie were as intense as lovers in their rivalry for the affection of Michael, but Michael Bennett would have been chosen by anyone on Broadway. Not by Allan Carr, though. Allan chose me. Imagine! Maybe to give the (manicured) finger to a Broadway that regarded him as a silly Hollywood queen; maybe because he sat through all those backer auditions and was impressed; maybe it simply was ego, insisting on backing the horse he entered the Broadway derby with. Whatever the reason, not another producer on Broadway would have done what he did. The God that loves loyalty among gays was pleased: Allan's loyalty paid off bigger than his dreams—and his dreams were enhanced by coke. *La Cage aux Folles* ran for four years, had several national companies, played London and Sydney, and made a fortune— more for Allan and his cronies than for his investors. He didn't come from Broadway and he never planned to stay on Broadway; maybe that's why he conquered Broadway.

Now to answer the unanswered questions above: who is responsible for what musical staging, etc. I didn't digress as an attempt to duck answering; the questions are too important. The basic underlying issue is director versus choreographer for control of the performance.

To risk an umbrella generalization, as a breed, choreographers are not too good with actors; consequently, they're not good at getting the performances that make musicals musical theatre rather than musical comedy. They're good with dancers, whom they understandably treat as bodies because they use them to create in the way authors use words and composers use notes. Actors have their own particular kind of creativity. They don't respond well to being used as putty. Even though in the end they may want to be told which way to go, they need to arrive at that point; they need to be treated as people. Even choreographers aware of that need have trouble getting an acting performance, because while they're fluent in the language of dancers, the language of acting is foreign to them. Their poetic metaphors are comprehensible (and flattering) to dancers; actors need less artistic and more specific speech to deal with subtext and unconscious emotions. The acting in the shining days of the choreographer/director shows was never quite as good as it could have been—not even in Fosse shows, which is odd, because the acting in his movies is very good. On the other hand, the acting in the movie of *West Side Story* is embarrassing (don't rely on memory, view it again, just the first ten minutes; you will be aghast at your younger judgment). The inept performances could be attributed to Hollywood's Robert Wise, who is screen-credited with co-directing the movie with Broadway's Jerome Robbins. Wise, a former film editor, was the lauded director of several woodenly acted films—the movie version of *The Sound of Music,* for example, was his. Jerry, who at least *asked* for assistance in directing the acting of the original stage *West Side,* shared the Oscar for it with Wise (even though he had been fired during the shooting). The overacting of the peroxided, Max Factored Jets can be attributed to him, but not the reciting of Richard Beymer. But which of them was responsible for the pancaked Sharks in silk blousons and their Day Gloed, Carmen Mirandaed girls? Small wonder that three decades later, high-school students in Amherst who had only seen the movie, not the show, said *West Side Story* was anti–Puerto Rican and blocked a projected school production.

Who is responsible for the smoke and mirrors? Varies. Who has the bigger name, the director or the choreographer? Who *wants* the responsibility? Who knows how to inspire designers? Who is more creative? That is the single most determining factor, as it should be. The single most important practical question is: who stages the songs—the director or the choreographer, or both in tandem? Even should it be the latter, it still will be who is first among equals, director or choreographer?

A bravura song in *Cage* called "A Little More Mascara" provides a perfect example of the difference between a director's approach and a choreographer's approach in the staging and performance in comparing the original production and the recent revival. In the original, Albin (George Hearn at his best) is sitting in his sad cubicle of a dressing room. The dressing room is in midair, isolating Albin, visually making him lonely and alone. He sits at his dressing table in a corset with the "false boobs" he sings about mournfully, without makeup (George's white-on-white skin helped), an aging queen staring into the mirror at his wrinkles. His star as Zaza, drag Queen of Riviera Cabaret, is flickering out. As he sadly sings, the only thing that keeps him going is to "put a little more mascara on." As he begins making up, he does just that: light base, eye shadow, false eyelashes, mascara. Brush on a touch of rouge, a little more mascara, lipstick, a little more mascara. Pull on a wig; pull up a gold-sequined dress hidden by the skirt of the dressing table; fasten it via a rhinestone collar (and Velcro); throw a feather boa around his powdered shoulders; step out from behind the dressing table, and lo and behold! There, on the top of a lighted stairway that slid out to greet him with an archway of twinkling lights coming down to frame him, there was Zaza! Undiminished, triumphant, Queen of the Riviera again! It was a highly theatrical staging and an emotionally moving performance.

The steps necessary to transform an aging old queen into a glamorous cabaret star before the eyes of the audience were worked out with mathematical precision. The application of each piece of makeup, the wig, the dress, the boa—all were carefully timed to the music. George rehearsed and rehearsed so that all the technical parts of the song didn't get in the way of what made it emotionally moving and finally thrilling: his acting, his performance. Albin started the song aging, discouraged, disheartened; the life force emerged and he began to get stronger, younger—transformed himself from a used-up has-been to a glamorous, invincible star. The song needed both elements to work, and it got them.

In the revival, Zaza—he was never Albin in "Mascara," only Zaza—also began in midair, on a platform in a glistening black gown against a black curtain. When he sang of putting "a little more mascara on," the involuntary question was, where? There wasn't conceivable room for more, or for a millimeter more makeup of any kind: he was slathered in it, it was inches thick, it looked heavier than the dress. Nor was there any attempt to progress from the "ugly duckling to a swan" the lyric described. The change he did make was to rip off the glistening black gown and—surprise?—a glittering black-sequin gown under-neath. What, then, was the song about? A change of costume. A camp number by just another drag queen, not a musical soliloquy by an aging artist determined to keep going. The choreographer responsible for the staging won the Tony that season.

The difference between the two approaches reflects the difference in the Broadway theatre at the time of each production. The twenty-first-century Broadway theatre shows Hollywood's influence—not just on musical theatre, on all theatre. The play is no longer the thing; the star is the thing. Musicals? Styled for the same audience as the multimillion-dollar blockbuster—one with neither heart nor mind. The Broadway blockbuster favors frenetic musical numbers with a thinly satirical connective tissue and a presumably saleable, presumably original element—a zoftig drag leading lady in *Hairspray*, for example. Actual originality, with a very occasional exception like *LoveMusik*, is found in transfers from Off Broadway like *Spring Awakening*. But even there, the originality is in the musical staging and the powerful rock music; the story, shocking in its long-gone day, is banal today, the bungled abortion is predictable, and the moaning that follows is merely sentimental slop to the new young audience rocking in its expensive seats to the music that brought it there. The heart and mind were not affected. Nor were they affected by the revival of *La Cage aux Folles*.

Question: over two decades earlier, did the Broadway theatre seek to touch the heart and provoke the mind? Often. Did the original production of *Cage*? Yes, the director surely did. Did he achieve what he wanted?

No, judging by the sneers of the activist gays during the first weeks of what was an enormous, unexpected hit. They loudly complained the show was vanilla, white bread, and timid, though beautiful to look at. (A year later, at an expensive fundraising gala dinner, the Human Rights Campaign, a premier gay organization, awarded Jerry, Harvey, and me their premier prize. Well, they needed names to sell the expensive tables.)

The view from the stage of the Palace Theatre differed from

that of the denigrators. The Cagelles in the opening number looked out and saw men burying their faces in their programs rather than look at other men in drag. At the end of the show, the Cagelles saw the same men on their feet applauding them. When I watched in the aisles to check the audience response, the white of Kleenex taken out of purses invariably caught my eye at the moment when Jean-Michel, juvenile and son, acknowledged Albin as his mother. Also sentimentality? At least an emotional response. At the beginning of the second act, there was a rather corny number in which musical-comedy Riviera sailors and waterfront types instructed Albin on how to be a man. Scott Salmon, whose choreography throughout the show was consistently remarkable, did what he could, but what can you do with however determined but still basically chorus boys pretending to be butch seamen? Director and choreographer then worked in tandem. George Hearn was given the image of a boy who had been called "faggot" all his life, and the dancers, who could identify, were the cowardly bullies kicking the sissy underdog. The number acquired not depth, as much as that was desired, but a dimension that removed it from the toothpaste-smiling world of musical comedy. The emotion was on the stage, not in the audience; but at least it was somewhere. In today's theatre, it is rarely anywhere.

The advent of AIDS took more of a toll on the company than on the box office—perhaps because of the absence of sex in the show; perhaps because of the fantastic costumes, which graced the show with an aura of unreality; perhaps because the audience didn't want to believe in the reality of the plague. Considering the preponderance of gays in the cast, the number of the afflicted was relatively small. The first to fall was a Cagelle who had steadfastly maintained he was straight. When he became infected, there was no schadenfreude; when he died, everybody mourned. No one was mourned more than Fritz Holt—executive producer to some, superb PSM to others, beloved by company, crew, everyone, closest of friends to me. One day he walked into my living room—it seems long ago and not so long ago—stretched out his six feet four inches on my couch, and opened his shirt. A port for AZT had been implanted in his chest.

"Do you want to live like that?" he said. "I don't." And he didn't. He went dancing at the Saint and continued to do drugs.

He was directing a national company of *Cage* when I got a phone call: "Fritz is sick." I went to rehearsal. I hadn't seen him in two weeks; I was told to be prepared—which, of course, was not possible. His long hair had fallen out in clumps, he had lost pounds—he was always wanting to lose weight, but not this much, this way—and his eyes were all terror. I gave a good performance; by then, I'd had a little practice. I took over rehearsals. Less than a week later someone came in and said Fritz was dead. I lost it then; everyone in the room did. We just sat for a moment, and then we went back to work—not because the show must go on, though it must and should, but because we didn't know what else to do.

Death always seems recent to me, I've lived through so many. The latest, Tom Hatcher from lung cancer, was really recent. We were together for fifty-two years. I'm unable to live through the empty space; I can only survive.

AIDS didn't end the run of *La Cage aux Folles*. What did end it was what began it. The air rights to the Palace Theatre, our home for four years, were sold to a chain that wanted to build a new hotel over the theatre. It was contractual time for construction to begin. The show had to move out, but that was fine: we were set to move to the Mark Hellinger. The Moonies, however, wanted the Hellinger for their tabernacle. They offered Allan Carr a lot of money—Allan, not the show, not his investors, his partners, his cronies; Allan. He took it, and that was the end of *La Cage aux Folles,* the musical. He was why it began; he was why it ended. It was always his show. He went back to his Ingrid Bergman house in Beverly Hills, where he waited to end his run.

Cage was a singular experience. As a director, I learned so much in a variety of areas, largely by taking chances and going where instinct told me to go. The most important learning usually comes from pain, but here it came from the opposite: the love that was as much a part of each company in this country and abroad as the title of the show. A simple life lesson: enjoy the work while you're doing it for the sheer pleasure of doing it. If you can be proud of the result, you've succeeded, no matter what happens. With *La Cage aux Folles,* I succeeded. Neither the show nor I will go down in any books (the Tonys roster doesn't count for me), but I succeeded and had an amazingly good time doing it.

P.S. Everyone made money.

SIX

Why?

"WHY DID I DO IT?" asks Rose. A familiar question at one time or another to anyone, including the director of a flop musical. After *Nick & Nora*, I asked myself why I did it. The answer was friendship—no, not excusable, but a trap for anyone in any role in the theatre. I also asked myself why I persisted with it even though Tom had told me it was doomed and I should stop. The answer to that was ego: *I* could get it on—I did. And *I* could get it to work—I couldn't. There are all sorts of reasons I would like to claim, like the show being dead in the water before it opened because of false allegations made in a carnivorous press during too many weeks of previews; but the fact is, the show flopped.

Now put the question in the present tense. Obviously, the actors have to ask: why is my character doing this? What about asking, Why am I singing? Why am I dancing? Those questions are for the director even if the authors have or think they have answered it. With *West Side Story*, however, those questions were never asked—not by the director, not by the cast, not by the audience, not by the critics, not by anyone, because we never asked them. We were telling much of the story through dancing and singing; it was a natural way to us, consequently it *was* natural. We did spend an inordinate amount of time seeking a name to describe what we were doing before we settled on "lyric theatre"— not too pretentious (or too meaningful), used in early interviews and then forgotten by all except the Library of Congress. There's a comfort in having a label identifying what you're doing when what you're doing doesn't quite fit in any category. Once it's over and done, it no longer needs a label. At least, what we had done didn't need any label for me. For me, we had come closer than I had thought possible to what we had dreamed. Time to move on to the next whatever it would be in whatever form.

Even before I began actually writing the book of *West Side Story*, when I was making an outline to structure the story, and thus give us something concrete to work from, I described the prologue as being danced with three or four spoken words. What better way to set the style, to tell the audience this story was going to be told primarily through music and dance?

That style was influenced to some extent by the fact that the choreography was to be by Jerome Robbins. Similarly, preceding the murderous rumble that ends the first act with a quintet sung by the whole company was influenced to a great extent because the music was to be by Leonard Bernstein. Lenny and Jerry were two of the most remarkable musical-theatre talents of that time, of any time. How could that not affect the style of the show?

Many say *West Side* forever changed the American musical—a claim made these days by shows like *Rent* and *Spring Awakening* with no visible proof—because of its use of dance and music. To me, it used those elements better than they had ever been used before; but what it really changed, what its real contribution to American musical theatre was, was that it showed that any subject—murder, attempted rape, bigotry—could be the subject of a popular musical.

Because of the conscious emphasis on music and dance, *West Side* had the shortest book of any musical to date. I became adept at providing the briefest of lead-ins to a song or number. In the second act, for example, Anita knocks on the door to the bedroom where Tony and Maria have just made love. Tony slips out the window; Maria opens the door. Anita comes in and looks at the bed. Maria says:

"All right! Now you know!"

Anita says: "And you still don't know! Tony is one of them!"—and sings, "A boy like that who'd kill your brother!"

Two lines and we're into a searing, climactic duet. Not bad, and helpful to the show, but a technical proficiency traceable to my beginnings in radio, where I learned economy in dialogue. What came just as easily but meant more to the show and was more gratifying to me was the obstacle that kept Tony from getting the crucial message about Maria. Instead of a delayed messenger as in Shakespeare, it was bigotry—a basic theme of the show. In Shakespeare's native country, that change received a great deal of attention; in this country, it went unnoticed. It provided the show's last use of music—the underscoring of the attempted gang rape.

Oddly enough for a show that relies so much on song and dance, there is neither in the last half of the second act. That was not intended. A long speech Maria has just before the end, I wrote as a dummy lyric for a final aria. Why no aria? Unfortunately, Lenny never found music that pleased him. To this day, Maria delivers that dummy lyric as an impassioned speech. So "masterpieces" are created.

Because of my belief that *West Side Story* should be done as it was done originally, I had no interest in directing any production. In 1980, there was a none-too-successful revival mastered by Jerry that didn't change my mind—it largely replicated the original, but it was bland. Yet in 1998, I redirected an English touring company headed for London. Why? Enter Freddie Gershon.

Freddie *is* MTI—Music Theatre International, the best company to handle subsidiary rights to musicals all over this country, Europe, Japan, South Africa, tomorrow the world. Freddie loves musical theatre and has made a life interest of bringing musical theatre to high-school kids, and vice versa. Following journalistic practice, I disclose that Freddie and his wife, Myrna, the high priestess of originality, can be counted among the best friends Tom and I ever had. MTI is still the leader in its field. But back to the English touring company.

It wanted to play London. A member of one of the estates in control of the rights to *West Side* saw the production and judged it ready. One of Freddie's people reported otherwise. Freddie, knowing I was going to be in England, suggested I see the touring company fast. I did—in Southampton—and put the transfer to London on hold. When I came home, I phoned Jerry: two weeks with Jerome Robbins, I reported, could make the company worthy of the transfer. Jerry was sick, much sicker than I suspected, too sick to direct. He asked if I would take over for him. That surprised me. Equally surprising, I agreed. Why all the surprise? Our personal relationship had been nonexistent for years.

We had met and become good friends during World War II— yes, that far back, and I'm still going. At the time we met, I was a sergeant in the army, writing radio propaganda; Jerry was a soloist in Ballet Theatre. He had a lot of friends and was a lot of fun. By happenstance—I knew nothing about ballet; my interest was in the person who took me—I was at the opening night of *Fancy Free*. Jerry didn't have quite as many friends after that overnight success. He became suspicious of people, and the theme of *Gypsy*—the need for recognition—buried his life. With me, however, he was still Jerry, not Jerome Robbins.

We were both in Hollywood when I met Tom and, for the moment, was resisting joining my life with his. Jerry more than approved of Tom, Tom was what I needed, but I was resisting and set to return to New York. Jerry forestalled that by insisting I stay with him—ostensibly to talk about *West Side Story*—in the Beverly Hills house he was renting while he did *The King and I* for the movies. That eliminated my excuse for having to go back to New York.

I have always remembered Jerry and me being close in those

days, but I didn't know how close until, clearing out some files, I came across a long letter from Jerry dated October 6, 1955. Instead of mailing it to me in New York, he was sending it via Tom, who was moving there to live with me, because he thought it would reach me faster. How slow was air mail in 1955?

"I will sure be sorry to see Tom leave," he wrote, "but as he says, what a wonderful Christmas we are all going to have together in New York and I do look forward to the fact that both of you will make New York a happier place to be in." Jerry Robbins wrote that, a Jerry Robbins I don't remember.

The Jerry I do remember turns up in what he writes about "ROMEO" (aka *West Side Story*)—how he has waited seven years for Lenny and me to sit down and start writing but he didn't mind because he wouldn't have wanted anyone else. And, much to my surprise, about my play *A Clearing in the Woods.* In his version, he loved the play and wanted badly to direct it but I held him off; in my version, he backed out of directing it. Which is true? How would I know?

The last paragraph of the letter is written by the Jerry Robbins who wrote the first, the Jerry I don't remember. "Write me, bubby *[sic]*, and tell me all. I envy you the Fall in New York, the life in Quogue, but I am happy for all the happiness that you will be having. With all my love, Jerry." Those *were* the days. Those *are* the days that we miss, that are the best, that we should never forget, but memory, like success, can be a spoiler.

When *West Side Story* finally happened and succeeded, Jerry's excessive need for recognition went into high gear, slowing down only when McCarthyism struck him. That added to the disintegration of our relationship, already under way. Those memories are too sharp.

On the occasion of a birthday party he was giving himself, he asked Nora Kaye, known variously as the Duse of the Dance or the

Red Ballerina and rumored at various times to be marrying Jerry and/or me: "Do I *have* to invite Arthur?"

When Ahmet Ertegun, the record mogul, gave him a party for his seventy-fifth birthday, Jerry called me at really the last minute and said grumpily: "I know you know it's the last minute but I'd like you to come." I went and had a good, if strange, time. It was a huge party at Maxim's in New York: black tie; champagne like tap water; two tables of show folk, two hundred tables of big money and big celebrities; an orchestra; dancing; entertainment; speeches; and—finally—Jerry. He spoke of late-nightly meetings with his neighbor Mica Ertegun, Ahmet's famous interior-decorating wife, as they walked their dogs, Jerry alone, always alone—"I'm a loner," he said wistfully. Sitting with the show folk was his ignored lover, Jesse Gerstein, a photographer. Phyllis Newman said, "If I had a gun, I'd shoot Jerry right now." Jesse died of AIDS at the age of thirty-four.

Our professional relationship wasn't smooth, but it was always characterized by mutual respect. He may have had to make himself drive over to my house in Quogue from his in Watermill to ask— Jerome Robbins *asking!*—for my help with his *Jerome Robbins' Broadway,* but drive over he did. The reunion wasn't without laughter. And tears, actual, visible, from him when I said I would trust him (about royalties). I gave him as much help as I could with his show, for which he was very appreciative.

When the gaggle of producers on *Nick & Nora* added my refusal to fire Tina Paul, our choreographer, to the weekly waterboarding they gave me, I called Jerry and asked if he would come see the show. Tina's work with a company of nondancers impressed him. And the show? He liked it, but . . . But what? Something, he didn't know what, was wrong. We talked at length, as only friends do. Neither of us could figure out what that something was, but there *was* something.

Too late, I figured out what it was; but it would have been too late at the outset. The musical was based on the *Thin Man* movies starring William Powell and Myrna Loy as Dashiell Hammett's famous characters Nick and Nora Charles. Except that by the time the musical was being birthed, Nick and Nora Charles weren't as famous as William Powell and Myrna Loy; in fact, they no longer existed. The world knew the *Thin Man* movies only as the lubricated adventures of William Powell and Myrna Loy. The actors in the musical, no matter how good Joanna Gleason and Barry Bostwick were—and they were very good—didn't have a chance. That was the something wrong with the show.

Why did I go to London to take over *West Side Story?* Jerry had come to help when I asked, I went when he asked. Happily, I wouldn't have two problems I had the last time I directed an English company of an American musical, *Gypsy* with Angela Lansbury: teaching the very insular English actors how to speak American and implanting them with energy. Twenty-five years later, the English (and Australians) could speak regional American and were capable of burning up the stage. Moreover—an important credential for playing *West Side*—there had been a large influx of people of color in Britain, so they all knew about prejudice, including their own. What that company didn't know was how to use what they did know in their performances—largely because they had been directed by an American choreographer practiced in putting out companies of *West Side Story* as by the established numbers.

The dancing was typical of what was wrong. It was advertised as Jerome Robbins's choreography, but it wasn't—it was his *steps*. What the steps meant, why they were doing them, the dancers were never told. The same was true of the songs, and as for the book—well, Maria and Tony were in love, Riff and Bernardo didn't like each other, and Anita was easily upset but had great extension. On the plus side, they were young, they were extremely attractive, they sang and danced beautifully, and they couldn't have been hungrier for help. In two weeks, they learned an enormous amount—and so did I.

From the misbegotten 1980 revival, I knew the scenery and costumes needed to be changed. The scenery, I couldn't do anything about, but I *could* light it differently. Directors should get down on their knees in gratitude to a lighting designer like Howell Binkley who did *Gypsy* with me and is doing the new *West Side Story* I'm preparing. The costumes, I could do something about—not enough, but something. It may have been authentic in 1957 for gangs to wear jackets to a dance, but in 1998, they looked like chorus boys. Out went most of the jackets, in came windbreakers and rolled-up shirt sleeves. With the girls, out came the scissors. Skirts were slashed from calf length to knee length and higher; necklines were lowered. It all helped.

A cardinal sin was committed: I fiddled with the choreography—beginning at the beginning with the first dance, the Prologue. A Jet, as choreographed, reaches over a wall to whack a Shark with a sack of flour; in London, he hit him over the head with a blackjack. I fiddled more with the dialogue—safe territory because that was mine. Most effective of all, and truest to life, Tony and Maria were as sexual as possible. They had absolutely beautiful voices, but to sing "Tonight" together, they had to get their tongues out of each other's mouth. In their bridal-shop scene, marriage seemed essential if what they were about to do was fruitful.

It was a very happy time for the cast, for me, and for the producers. I also learned about the pitfalls in *West Side Story:* some brought on by the passage of time were anticipated, some that I had thought were there weren't, some I hadn't realized were there were always there. More than anything else, I learned that what was most needed for any new production was a fresh, original look at the show. What that was, I had no idea. In 1998 in London, it didn't matter. The audience was too delighted to see the show done again and with passion and excitement to boot. In 2006 in New York, a new idea mattered.

In that year, there was a frenzied campaign for a revival of *West Side Story* on Broadway in 2007. Why? Presumably, to honor its fiftieth anniversary, but not incidentally that anniversary was a good selling point, not only for Broadway but for a subsequent tour, both of which could mean a lot of money. Money was the first priority in the country. Well, isn't theatre supposed to reflect the time?

There were two certified choreographers to choose from for the golden dancing goose, but who to direct? Who to be responsible for the production? The question was unsettled, settled, unsettled in meeting after meeting of the rights-holding estates until it was fortunately too late to get any production ready in time for the anniversary. During all the backing-and-forthing, however, something remarkable happened. That much-needed-and-wanted fresh, original approach to a revival had surfaced. It came from Tom Hatcher.

Tom always had a project going in addition to his day job. The most lasting was the beautiful twelve-acre private park he created in Quogue, where we would sit on a special bench every day and talk. Even now, every day I'm in Quogue, I sit on that bench and talk to him.

A less grand project was his prescient desire to learn Spanish. He worked hard at it, spending two weeks in Ecuador, where Quito has the best Spanish-teaching school in the world. As he became fluent, he travelled South America avidly and regularly. I went with him occasionally—love is togetherness, but it benefits from separation now and then. In Buenos Aires, we became friends of F&F—Federico and Fernando, agents, translators, facilitators, entrepreneurs. They knew everybody, were known by everybody and not quite placeable by anybody except those at the American embassy who knew Federico in his other life as the

Argentinean cultural and legal adviser. In the theatre, anything in English went into Spanish courtesy of F&F. They were eager to get a production of *West Side Story* done in South America, in Buenos Aires. One was done, but not in Buenos Aires, in Bogotá, and not by them.

I had been to Bogotá with Tom, but when that *West Side* was done by a local company in Spanish, he was there alone on opening night. He reported back on the production in excited detail. What most fascinated him was that the hometown language being Spanish, the Sharks were the heroes and the Jets were the villains. That sent mind and blood racing.

"If we could equalize the gangs here," I said, "both would be the villains they are."

"Why not have the Sharks speak Spanish?" Tom said.

And there it was—the reason for a new production. It excited me and now I wanted to direct it.

It excited everyone who heard Tom's idea. At first, I didn't tell them it was Tom's—I didn't want it dismissed. We had removed ourselves from the social world of the theatre a long time before, because he was dismissed as my "boyfriend." Liked and enjoyed, even lusted for, but victim of an attitude highlighted in my play *2 Lives:* when he fetched a drink for someone at a party, the person who had asked for it was gone when he came back. Subterranean homophobia is as strong as, perhaps even stronger than, its racial equivalent.

Working out the use of Spanish wasn't as simple as anticipated. Anita sings how much she wants to be an American. She would therefore sing in English, not Spanish—the jokes in the lyric of "America" wouldn't work in Spanish, anyway. She would also be determined to speak English even to Bernardo, who would be equally determined to speak Spanish. That would need revisions. So would the section in the dance hall when Bernardo speaks to Maria. It would be in Spanish, which Tony would not understand, though he would get the gist. And when Bernardo is killed, it's the end of English for Anita: "A Boy Like That" has to be sung in Spanish.

The challenge revved me up, but I couldn't handle it alone; I wasn't bilingual. I hadn't anticipated the need to, because Tom was so fluent in Spanish. He would be there to help as I worked on the script and in rehearsal as I worked on the performances. And then he wasn't there. He died of lung cancer on October 26, 2006. Fifty-two completely shared years. Loss is hard, it's difficult, it's sometimes impossible, but, as I slowly learned, I was fortunate to have those fifty-two years.

"The show must go on" isn't always just a joke or a cliché. *West Side Story* literally did have to go on. It was already contracted for; after a pause for the *Gypsy* Tom had urged me to do—a year's pause because of its move to Chernobyl, aka Broadway—work began, though with not as much enthusiasm. I ran into difficulty trying to get a script in Puerto Rican Spanish. MTI had one, but it looked as though it had barely survived tropical dry rot. Another script turned up that was in Spanish, not necessarily Puerto Rican, but scenes were missing. I suspended hunting and called F&F. They had always wanted to do *West Side,* they were friends, they had to have a script of *West Side Story* in Spanish.

They did. It had been vetted by Tom, and his corrections were on it in his familiar handwriting.

A director's work begins long before the first day of rehearsal—at the moment he opens the script. Which will be different by the first day of rehearsal, even for a revival. For me, with *West Side Story,* work obviously began even before that due to the bilingual factor. Tom's death was an unexpected rupture that diminished my enthusiasm for the project, but the arrival of his script, corrected in his handwriting, was a message that sent me back to work with more than just renewed enthusiasm. I went back with the love that drove *Gypsy.*

Although I set about cobbling together the bilingual version myself, someone was going to be needed to vet my questionable Spanish. It was Kevin McCollum who suggested asking Lin-Manuel Miranda, who was busy preparing the transfer of their *In the Heights* from Off Broadway to Broadway. Nevertheless, Lin readily agreed to help. Who were these people, and why were they so helpful?

There are no coincidences or accidents, but there is often one hand washing the other, and occasionally even an act of pure generosity. Kevin and his partner, Jeffrey Seller, were producers of Lin's musical about Puerto Rican Americans in far uptown New York City, as well as the executive producers, partnered with the Nederlanders, of this new bilingual version of a musical set not as far uptown on the west side of New York. But Lin? Why did he agree without hesitation? A partial answer: he was brought up on *West Side Story,* he admired and respected it and always had. But there is the rest of the answer: Lin-Manuel Miranda is a generous young man, in an old-school tradition that is almost gone.

Even while working on the script, a director is mentally assembling the team to bring his vision of the play to theatre life. For *West Side,* my choice would obviously be the same team that worked so brilliantly on *Gypsy,* and it was, but any director with sense and/or experience knows there's a good chance he will be thrown a curve. I was thrown two.

The first and more important was by Craig Jacobs, but that I understood. He was burned out. *Gypsy* had been difficult enough, *West Side Story* was going to be more difficult—because of the way I envisioned the production—and he wanted to go back to *Phantom of the Opera,* where he had been production stage manager for eleven years. He had been on loan to *Gypsy* from Hal Prince, *Phan-*

tom's director and an old friend of mine dating back to the original production of *West Side,* where he was the most active producer. But I went even farther back with his inestimable wife, Judy, the only person I would eagerly have lunch with. I knew her from early Hollywood when she palled around with her imaginary friend, Bessie Glum, and I wrote a play for her twelfth birthday called *Queen Lear* which had only one speaking part—Judy's.

Craig would still check performances of *Gypsy* twice a week. Most helpful of all, he would do what I most needed him for and what he did better than anyone in the theatre: he would make out the schedule for *West Side Story* from its first day of rehearsals through its tryout in Washington. That was going to be tortuous and tricky, previewing through the Christmas holidays up to pre-Inauguration frenzy, all during days of financial yo-yo hysteria to prevent a Depression.

The second curve was thrown by Marty Pakledinaz, and was a clean hit to the heart. On *Gypsy,* only Craig had been closer to me. During the time between City Center and the St. James Theatre, Marty and I had continued discussing the theatre we wanted to be part of and talked about *West Side Story* as that kind of theatre. However, Marty had an offer from another director he "loved" to do a quasi-new musical—"quasi" because the score was old Gershwin songs and the show was being star-tailored. The two shows were scheduled for the same rehearsal date. Marty chose the quasi. What I didn't understand and still don't was Martin Pakledinaz choosing that kind of theatre.

Before Tom's death, I would have been angry at Marty. Now I felt disappointed that the friendship was over. Too unforgiving? The loss of Tom has made me treasure the few true friends I am fortunate to have; admittedly, they are few. A friend cannot be replaced; a designer, even one as good as Marty, can be. His replacement was David Woolard, a man whose work I had never seen. Why did I choose him? Well, I knew of no other costume designer right for the job; I interviewed two or three and wasn't encouraged. But David was highly recommended by Jim Youmans and Howell Binkley of the *Gypsy* team, who had worked with him before and often. I knew Jim and Howell well, I trusted them, and they were choosing a designer they would have to work with. A team that likes working as a team is essential for a director.

When I met David, we connected almost from the moment he sat upright yet relaxed on my sofa. He's laid-back where Marty is always on the verge of something jittery. The decision was cinched when after I explained how I saw the production, David used one telling word to describe how he saw the costumes: *dangerous.* With, once again, Dan Moses Schreier, the best of sand designers, the *West Side Story* team was complete.

A DVD of a highly praised fiftieth-anniversary revival of *West Side* confirmed for me that the passage of time had made it even more of a minefield than I had thought ten years earlier when I directed it in London. Why? Because, an accurate replication of the original, it showed too clearly that the most difficult problems stemmed from portraying the Jets as likeable tough little thugs. This misconception was reflected in the opening Jet song, staged as a fifties musical-comedy number, and in "Gee, Officer Krupke," a vaudeville comedy showstopper. The kids in gangs today are angry, vicious, and violent, heedless killers, but they were in the fifties, too. They haven't changed, the theatre has. Somehow, they would have to be played as what they are.

Then there was the second-act ballet. As beautiful as much of the dancing is, no matter how you slice it, the second-act ballet is still the second-act ballet. Lovely dancing with a generalized emotion or two in a self-conscious dreamworld. Half a century ago, it was part of the show; today, it has to be made part of the play. Not an easy task, but hopefully achievable if a very different approach is used. A challenge, all this, for me to communicate to Joey McNeely, who has been replicating Jerry's choreography for years all over Europe as well as here, and for him to execute with his assistant, the lovely Lori Werner. They are perfectly balanced: Joey is constantly fired up, ready to take off; Lori is his control tower.

The new approach was equally difficult and became more so each day for Patrick Vaccariello, the music conductor, who was totally tuned in to what I wanted played and sung differently in *Gypsy* and achieved it brilliantly. I can't envision doing a musical without Patrick. That music, however, was Jule Styne; this was Leonard Bernstein, much more complex and sacrosanct. The fine line that had to be walked with this new approach, erasing the fifties without violating what made *West Side Story* the classic it has become, was a new approach I explained at a production meeting of the whole team.

Production meetings are the most fertile ground for the ideas that transform a show. They can pop suddenly out of anyone's mouth to influence, shift, elevate the direction of the show. At one early meeting, I heard someone who turned out to be me explain a conception as though it were the result of much thought but in reality had just occurred to me that minute. Why? I have no idea, and since it's decades since I was in analysis, no therapist to help. *West Side Story* was about how love cannot survive in a world of bigotry and violence. It exists, then, in a world of its own—a Renaissance world, the world of Romeo and Juliet, the greatest love story ever told and retold. It wasn't necessary to relate all this; just the word "Renaissance" excited the room. Everyone got it and used it. The fire escape that Tony climbs to reach Maria became a baroque balcony that resembles a fire escape. The color of Tony and Maria's costumes reflects the Renaissance: a Della Robbia blue rather than a Jet or Shark color.

We had a three-hour production meeting on the subject of color. In the original production, and thus in almost every production since, the Sharks were in purple, red, and black, the Jets were in blue and yellow. Solid colors made the dance at the gym vividly theatrical in 1957. Today, that highly lauded treatment would make the gangs and their girls seem like chorus boys and girls. David Woolard devised a new approach. The color that individualized each gang was on each costume but in many different ways—some large, some small, even as small as a headband or a scarf around the neck, but the gang alliance was clear. Life imitated art when in Nyack, Jim Youman's hometown, a high-school girl wearing a neck bandana the color of her boyfriend's gang had it yanked off by a member of a rival gang. In less than ten minutes, war broke out with knives and even axes. No killings but several hospitalizations. The immediate cause: color.

At the first meeting of the whole production team, I claimed two things were going to make this *West Side Story* unique and unlike any other that had ever been done anywhere. First, of course, was that it was going to be bilingual. I didn't realize, however, until auditions, when scenes were read in Spanish, that the difference was going to be even more dramatic than Tom and I had imagined. Latinos are more passionate and less inhibited than gringos or Anglos or whatever hyphenated immigrants you want to label the rest of us. Even read with script in hand, their scenes were on fire, and funny even without understanding the actual words. The Jets were going to have to dig deep to hold their own. That led directly to the second element that was going to make this *West Side Story* so special.

Beginning with the original production, dancing and singing were always the focus, the centerpiece. Who hasn't seen a production where the dancing or singing or both weren't breathtaking? But who has ever seen a production where the acting was more than passable, let alone good? Why? Because except for Chino and the four adults, the cast was chosen first for their ability as dancers and/or singers, second for their looks, and last, if they could read lines and make some sense. In this production, the ability to act was going to be on a par with the ability to dance and sing, but the emphasis in rehearsal and performance was going to be—heresy!—on acting.

The effect was felt everywhere. I tested the singing of the Jet Song with Cody Green, a brilliant dancer auditioning for Riff, by asking him to sing the lyric, not with fifties musical-comedy charm but with the icy command of a potential killer. He wasn't fazed; there was an actor there. He tried, it worked, and Patrick assured me he could help with the orchestra.

"Krupke" wasn't going to be as easy: comic vaudeville is hard to justify. I had figured out how to get into the song and hoped to work out the rest in rehearsal. "Hope" is the operative word. Staring at the drop of the fence in front of which "Krupke" was going to be performed was the opposite of inspiring. It seemed like musical comedy but I didn't know what it should be and was stymied until David Saint, my associate director, said, "Why don't we lose the drop and play the scene and the song in the main set?" He was referring to the stunning depiction of a harsh and brutal neighborhood, a breeding ground for violence that sets the tone of the production. There was no way "Krupke" could be a vaudeville comedy in that grim world, but half a dozen other ways it could be played came immediately to mind.

Acting gives meaning—to every note and every step as well as to every word. Acting was what made *Gypsy* so much more than it ever had been. Acting, I hoped, would do the same for *West Side Story*, even with less opportunity and more obstacles. If the right actors could be found.

The casting demands of *West Side Story* are greater than those of any musical ever written. Can you dance? Not hip-hop, not just move, but dance, including ballet? Can you sing Bernstein—a range from musical comedy to opera—with a trained voice and vocal cords that weren't abused by the distorted sound and bent notes required for shows like *Spring Awakening* and *Rent* and

Wicked? (It's disheartening how many talented young singers have abused their vocal cords so badly that unless they get proper training quickly, they probably won't be able to sing at all in a few years.) Can you act? Not indicate, not show and tell what you are feeling, but feel it so strongly inside that the audience will get it? And for this time, are you Latino? Not just dark-haired with high school Spanish but authentically Latino? If not, two sentences into a scene with an authentic Latino reader and a ringer is embarrassingly exposed. Minorities had been misled so many times that when it became clear that we were serious about casting Latinos as Latinos, the word spread throughout the overjoyed Latino community so fast that the casting people were overwhelmed.

I was also determined to get a really young company. The original production hadn't been overly concerned with age. Kenny Leroy, who was an otherwise admirable Bernardo, had to be asked to excise from his program bio that he had been in the original production of *Oklahoma!* Up close, our Bernardo, George Akram, originally from Venezuela, was a boy, but he had such an intense stillness, so commanding a presence, so quietly burning a sexuality—the girl who read with him kept caressing her chest—that he seemed a man three times his age. But George was not only exceptional, he was an exception. For the leading parts, one after another teenage dancer or singer was unfortunately unbelievable; they not only looked unused as teenagers can but they had no experience in their lives to draw from to play the characters. Their gang-member-in-life equivalents, teenagers though they be, look a used thirty, small wonder with the experience in their brutal lives. "Really young" became a casting casualty; twenty-five and over a necessary compromise.

Matt Cavanaugh is not twenty-five, but if he is a compromise, I'll take one like him every time. Tony is older than the other Jets and Matt looks younger than he is and as good as Tony should look. He is an actor and has a voice that is not only beautiful but an anomaly these days: it's really trained. He also has a depth and passion I suspect he didn't know he had that exploded during rehearsals, exposing his vulnerability and enabling me to make the play what it was always meant to be but never quite was: the story of *Tony* and Maria.

We had no Maria. Hundreds of girls had been seen but there was only one possibility. She had every quality needed for the role except the one that couldn't be compromised: she wasn't Latino. It was regrettable, especially to me, because she was an exceptionally good actress. Unfortunately, the only thing about her that was Latino was her high school Spanish.

Every city in the country having been combed and still no Maria, the casting calls went out to Spain, Cuba (worry about the State Department later), Mexico, and South America, except Argentina. Argentina was mine; Argentina, which meant Buenos Aires, with its own Broadway for American musicals in Spanish and two schools of musical theatre and F&F. I called them.

As usual, Federico said Tom was taking care of me, and apparently was up to date because F&F did indeed have a Maria. The perfect Maria, according to Federico, at the moment appearing as the beautiful bitch in *Hairspray*. That didn't strike me as much of a recommendation for *West Side Story* and Leonard Bernstein—pace Tom—but I was told I could judge for myself: the perfect Maria was on YouTube. YouTube. In 1957, when we couldn't find the perfect Tony or the perfect Maria, there wasn't even the Internet, but in 2008 on YouTube there was a girl named Josefina Scaglione. One viewing, and instinct said she would be our Maria: incredibly beautiful, with an incredibly beautiful voice, and incredibly, beautifully young.

She taped a DVD for us, singing "Tonight" in English sublimely and acting the first bridal-shop scene in English impressively, particularly considering who was playing Anita behind the camera—Federico Gonzales of F&F. The producers flew her to New York to audition. In person, she was even more perfect: more beautiful, a trained singer, a trained actress, a trained dancer, bilingual, charismatic, could take direction, and was just twenty-one, a girl in this country. But Buenos Aires is a European city; at twenty-one, Josefina was a young woman, not the lemonade girl she looked like, and in touch with her deepest emotions. She could go unexpected places as an actress and she did: in rehearsal she turned out to be an inventive comedienne. Directing her was a joy and a lesson. Since she was fluent in English, I forgot my own experience when I lived in Paris and had been fairly fluent in French (not anymore, alas). Is anyone totally fluent in a second language without living for years where it is the first language? I didn't watch my idioms with Josefina so there were times when she would say: "Arthur, I haven't understood one word you said for the last three minutes." I had to laugh. The whole company and crew adore her.

With one exception, the show was cast. Joey McKneely, who is meticulous and demanding, auditioned every dancer available until he was satisfied he had the best. But why not? *West Side Story* is considered a dance show, and at that point I still thought it was. The leading dancing role, Anita, still hadn't been cast. The original Anita, Chita Rivera, had every step she danced choreographed for her by Peter Gennaro, who knew her special talent and exploited it. Anita not only had to dance that strongly in the first act but to sing and act with even more power in the second. Small wonder we were a week from rehearsal with no Anita and seriously worried. Then came a candidate who had to be persuaded to audition.

Karen Olivo dazzled me the first time I saw her, which was Off-Broadway in Lin Miranda's *In the Heights*. She was a dancer but not of the caliber needed for Anita. She knew Joey McKneely felt that, and was hesitant about auditioning. But she very much wanted to play Anita. When Karen read, I looked at David Saint: this was an actress. But more: you looked at her even if she merely stood there and seemingly did nothing—"seemingly" because there was always something felt and true to the character going on inside her. I asked her to make an adjustment to how she was playing the scene. She did, easily. She sang "A Boy Like That" with a voice that matched her fury. She sang in English but she was bilingual and could have sung in Spanish if the lyric had been available. I needed to find out one thing more. I asked her if she would mind singing the song again but this time not angrily, as it had been done originally, as it is always done, but with the pain Anita must be feeling because Bernardo had just been killed. She took a moment, and then sang. By the end of the song, without any vocal or physical histrionic, she was in tears, everyone in the room was close to tears, and I had decided Karen Olivo had to play Anita. Then she danced for Joey.

Joey admired Karen for having the guts to audition for him, knowing what little regard he had for her dancing, and said he would do everything possible to help her dance the role. When Karen read the audition scenes, there wasn't one reading I had ever heard in my head but they were hers and they were right for her Anita. I thought, but didn't say, that if she couldn't dance Anita as choreographed by Peter Gennaro for Chita Rivera, then Joey McKneely would have to rechoreograph it for Karen Olivo—she was that important to the play.

When I looked at "America," the big dance number in the first act for Anita and the girls, that phrase "Anita and the girls" expressed exactly what I realized "America" was in *West Side Story*: a musical comedy would-be show-stopper that had nothing to do with Tony and Maria or the play. *West Side*'s dances were credited with moving the story forward. The dances were brilliant as dances, but "America" interrupted the story, it didn't move the story anywhere anymore than the famous prologue did. That was meant to establish the background for the gang war but what it established first was that the show was driven by dance. All the dances, I gradually realized, had to be examined to see if they really did contribute to the story—my goal was a musical play rather than a danced retelling of a legendary tale. If they didn't contribute, something had to be done to draw them into the play. I began with the prologue.

The opening music is threatening, as set originally and always replicated since; so is the tableau of the Jets on which the curtain rises. Then they start to dance, and in one minute the arms get soft and balletic, the emotions general, threat and gangs are gone, we are into dance-in-blue-jeans and there, by and large, we stay. A sequence meant to show the gang exulting in owning its turf may have looked just that in 1957; in 2008, it looks like musical comedy chorus boys stepping out, as they do in the movie. A Shark knocked to the floor by a Jet spits across the whole stage, his saliva hits the offending Jet on the back of his neck, the Jet turns and leaps on the Shark. That bothered me even in 1957; it had to be replaced with something stronger—a knife. A Jet whacking a Shark with a sack of flour now whacks him with a baseball bat. Even before all that, when the curtain rises, what the audience sees is a very different opening to a very different show.

Only the familiar brief, opening musical figure, as the curtain shoots up on that brutal set. Silence as out of the shadows steps Riff, a Cody Green with a cold, insolent look from hooded eyes. He slowly comes down to the edge of the stage, a Pied Piper for his Jets, who follow like rats down fire escapes, out of holes in a broken tenement, following Riff until they are all at the edge of the stage, glaring at the audience as though to say: "This is ours. Cross the line to come here and we'll cut your balls off."

The Jets have been set up as potential killers and that's how they dance. When Bernardo and the Sharks arrive to test whether they can cross the line safely, the menace increases and keeps increasing. The Shark no longer spits, he throws a knife across the stage, missing the Jet who now really leaps on the Jet to kill. When A-rab's ear is pierced, the dance moment when all the Sharks turn melodramatically away from A-rab to raise their arms, reaching for God-knows-what, is now all of them raising their fists to beat A-rab to a pulp. The steps are the steps danced over fifty years ago but there is no soft line, only hard angles, and the purpose and the meaning of the steps have been changed by the attitude of the angry, vicious gang members dancing them. The prologue now establishes the brutal world of the story.

"America" was altered more radically, but that change stemmed from a discovery about the lyric. Early in the play, in her first scene with Maria in the bridal shop, Anita's refusal to speak Spanish is set up along with her ability to intimidate other Puerto Ricans into speaking English. This sets up "America" being sung in English— as it has to be for all the jokes to work. The pattern of the song is that Rosalia, who wants to retun to Puerto Rico, sings a verse about something she misses there and is put down by Anita with the tag line. Then Anita sings of what she likes about America and sings the tag line herself.

Seeking a way to make "America" more than a number and pull it into the play, I examined the lyric and immediately saw something that had made sense when "America" was just a dance number. No, as a song in a play, it contradicted itself. If Anita really liked America, as she sang in each verse, why did she end the verse knocking America? Her first verse, for example, praises "everything free in America" but then adds "for a small fee in America." When I asked Steve Sondheim what he intended Anita's attitude to be when she sang this contradiction, his half-laughing, half-embarrassed answer exemplified what can happen in musicals over time when proper attention has not been paid. In rehearsal, "America" had been set by Peter Gennaro for Anita and Bernardo and the Shark boys and girls. Jerry took Bernardo and the boys out of the number. The tag lines like "for a small fee in America" had been Bernardo's retort to Anita. They were simply transferred to Anita and since Chita's dancing was the purpose of the number, she wasn't singing as a character. A joke was a joke and on to higher kicks.

The way to make "America" part of the play was now clear. It was an aspect of the inner conflict among Latinos, a friendly, comic battle between pro-American Anita, supported by her girl-friends, and pro–Puerto Rican Rosalia, supported by one cousin. The song and the dance were now done by people, characters in the play, not by performers in a number. Joey McKneely was adept at saving much of the choreography while at the same time adding enough to bring the dance into the story and suit Karen's Anita. But he wasn't satisfied. With style and simplicity, he justified the dancing as part of a musical *scene* which also allowed Karen to use more of her individual dazzle.

Joey's real triumph was with the second-act ballet that had never satisfied Jerry Robbins himself. Every day of the out-of-town tryout, Jerry had changed the ballet, often ordering new back-drops. (One looked like the Jersey swamps.) Joey re-created the ballet beautifully, it couldn't have been better danced, not even by the New York City Ballet, which regularly performs a *West Side Story Suite,* a popular success as ballet world, a pallid facsimile as theatre. It wasn't easy not to say anything with the company wait-ing after Joey showed me his version. I took him and Lori into another room and said it: "Joey, it's a dance concert. It has nothing to do with this *West Side Story.*"

We had talked earlier of what he considered his responsibility—to be faithful to Jerry's choreography—and what I considered mine—to be as faithful as I could to the original everything but to change what I felt was essential to give *this West Side Story* a reason for living. That had already been done with two problematic songs. The conversion of the opening "Jet Song" from a fifties musical-comedy number to the credo of a vicious gang had begun with Cody Green at his audition; it was comparatively easily com-pleted in rehearsal. "Gee, Officer Krupke" was an obstacle course I could only blame on myself. I had insisted on a comedy number in the second act to relieve the tension, invoking Shakespeare and his porter scenes to convince the others. In the uncinematic, mangled, and also anti–Puerto Rican movie, its position was shifted to the first act, which turned the gang even more into musical comedy chorus boys. Steve, who had advocated the switch, switched himself, saying it belonged back in the second act. But it didn't belong in this second act as the smack-out vaudeville red-nosed clown comedy-show stopper it was in the original. In this second act, the murder of two friends was deeply felt and acknowledged. How could "Krupke" be sung without ignoring that? By the attitude of the first singer—Action, the angriest member of the gang. He's already been to the police station and made fools of the police. His singing is delighted defiance, which disgusts A-rab. He and his cohort, Big Deal, use Baby John as a puppet as they do the song. Nothing is a vaudeville turn, everything is an over-the-top put-down of everything society upholds. There is no choreography; it's a musical scene where the gang members explode with black humor, which finally draws even A-rab in.

As difficult as "Krupke" had been to make part of the play, the second-act ballet was much more so. When I detailed to Joey what I thought might make the ballet not a ballet, he moved fast, too fast at first, but always on the right track. Incorporating specifics like having a grubby street kid sing "Somewhere" and ending the song and what was the ballet with Tony and Maria, turned out to be the key to what was and is Joey's triumph. Jerry's ballet steps are still there but they now have a purpose and an emotional center. Call it the second-act ballet, call it "Somewhere," call it whatever you will, but it now has meaning, it's moving, it belongs in the play, and for the first time it's part of the love story.

All these changes plus, of course, the addition of Spanish, make this *West Side Story* obviously unlike any other. But what makes it deeper and richer, really different, is something that probably will go unnoticed by most people: it is *acted,* and acted extremely well, by the entire company, from dancers without a line (but many an ad-lib) to the major characters—not merely as never before but as well as any nonmusical actors of any stature could. And it's all established in the first intimate scene, the so-called ladder scene that introduces Tony and "Something's Coming."

That scene, between Tony and Riff, is the first love scene in a play about love in a world of violence and bigotry. It has always been played fast and a bit coyly, primarily as a lead-in to a two-four that isn't quite a two-four and falls short as does the scene. Examine it, dig into it as one would with a scene in a play, and it becomes wrenching and essential to the telling of the story. It is a love scene that establishes the time and the theme of the play.

Each boy needs the other, but Tony no longer loves Riff as he did. Probably, at that age, there was some homoerotic element, but it's the love that's important. Riff's love for Tony explains why he keeps covering for him with the gang, keeps him in the gang when he knows Tony isn't and doesn't want to be, even gets killed because of that love. The tough leader of the gang in the preceding scene is here the vulnerable lover. Tony is a little older and has left boyhood and adolescent love. But we must know that he loved Riff to believe he is capable of the love that is on its way. A few cuts to eliminate quasi-boyishness and too much invented language, the scene now leads directly into "Something's Coming" as the reason for what we have just witnessed: the end of a love affair. It isn't a two-four, it's a growing discovery of who Tony is through his discovery of what he is hoping for.

That treatment eliminates the usual cuteness in the next scene, where Maria and Anita are introduced, and continues into the Dance at the Gym, where Tony and Maria meet. Played by Matt Cavanaugh and Josefina Scaglione, the nonliteral dialogue spoken during a slow cha-cha becomes, for the first time, a sexually charged love scene. And when Tony sings "Maria" two minutes later, it is not with reverence for a name, he is not a tenor in church singing of a virgin Maria, he is a lover, his passion exploding in variations on her name. Fortunately I didn't know, until Patrick told me, that what I was asking of Matt Cavanaugh was extremely challenging. His singing seems so effortless; there is never the feeling that so often occurs when "Maria" is sung—"Oh, God, will he hit that note?" He wasn't about hitting notes, he was about the emotion inside him. The aria—that's what it is—didn't end as it had before; it ended with a series of full, passionate "Maria"s followed by a gentle affirmation of Tony's love. Then, just before the last bars, he turns—and there is Maria on her balcony. It is to her that he sings that last, high pianissimo "Maria."

When he climbs up to Maria's fire-escape balcony, they immediately are lost in a passionate kiss. They can't keep their hands off one another, can barely stop kissing long enough to sing "Tonight," but they do, in voices belonging to a dream Tony and Maria who look the way a dream Tony and Maria should look, sing as they should sing, act as they should act. The love story is secured and the audience belongs to the lovers.

The initial reason for reviving *West Side Story* was that it would be bilingual. It is and it brings an exciting quality never before seen in musical theatre. But there was another dynamic that came later and was equally unique: the emphasis on acting. That brought the theme—love can't survive in a world of bigotry and violence—vividly to life with an emotional reality that was unexpectedly moving because of the acting of the entire company. *West Side Story* was lifted to a new level—the level *Gypsy* reached, the level I believe the musical play should reach.

In 1957, the first public performance of *West Side* was given at the National Theatre in Washington, D.C. Fifty-one years later the first public performance of a new, different *West Side Story* was given at the National Theatre in Washington, D.C. The theatre was not as I remembered it; actually, both the building and the décor of the theatre had changed. The show itself was not as those who had seen the original remembered it. It, too, had changed but many of those who claimed to have seen it hadn't seen what they remembered seeing. Most had really only seen the movie, which I wished they hadn't. None of that mattered. The first performance told us what mattered: it was greeted with a roar of approval.

Enthusiasm grew with each performance; the standing ovations came earlier and earlier.

It's infinitely easier to work on a show—and every show needs work—when the audience adores it and tickets are selling like mad, especially when foreclosure and bailout are the watchwords of the day. Easier to polish the performance, easier to deal with problems. There are always problems; and first on my list were the supertitles I hadn't thought necessary.

They ran in white on black rectangles on either side of the proscenium, a constant distraction whether read or not, because those flashing of white in every scene where a word was in Spanish pulled the audience out of the play. A bilingual script was meant to make the play exciting; instead, it was destroying it with those titles.

Some of this was because more had been translated into Spanish than I had intended, and I had been too lax (aka dumb) to realize this. "Rumble," most obviously, had been translated as "puela," which means "fight" in Spanish. Why? The Sharks spoke English, they would have said "rumble." Anita makes a point of speaking English while Bernardo insists on speaking Spanish. Her big speech to Bernardo in the scene before "America" was mistakenly in Spanish. It would be easy to restore it to English, but it was the whole approach, the insistence that supertitles were necessary, that had to be addressed. Making the decision unilaterally, I threw them out.

There was curiosity, anticipation, excitement before that first no-title performance. "Rumble" had replaced "puela," and I had inserted some English where I thought it necessary to help the story or to let the audience know what a scene was about. In the scene before "I Feel Pretty," Maria said in English, "Tonight is my wedding night." Her scene with Chino, which follows, was all in Spanish except for his last line said in English, the language of the traitor: "He killed your brother." Its impact after only Spanish was devastating.

The audience reaction left no doubt: the titles were removed permanently. "I Feel Pretty" stopped the show as it always had, but for the first time the scene with the duet of "A Boy Like That" and "I Have a Love," followed by a brief passage in English with Schrank, got a hand it had never gotten before. I had also cut the projections used during the Balcony Scene and "One Hand, One Heart." As a result of the double stripping down, the audience was totally involved the entire evening, surely the purpose of a play. There were always standing ovations at the end; usually not until major players took their bow. On the night the supertitles were eliminated, the entire audience stood up the moment the curtain rose after the play ended. Sweet validation.

Why? is the most important of questions, certainly the most important a director can ask. Beginning with himself: why is he a director? Not having any desire myself to direct, I was pressed into service during the dress rehearsal of my first play, *Home of the Brave*. The director, Michael Gordon, was feuding bitterly with Ralph Alswang, the scenic designer, over a window shade. Mike would order the stage manager—Jimmy Gelb, a Chekhovian character he knew from the Group Theatre—to lower the shade and shadow the room; Ralph would sneak on stage to raise the shade and let light in the room. Up, down, up, down—until an exhausted, exasperated Mike ran up the aisle of the Belasco Theatre and went screaming into the night. Who was to take over? Jimmy suggested me. The play was a war play, I wasn't long out of the army, I was still in my twenties and this was Broadway, but no one else offered. I had been troubled by Mike treating what I called "GI dialogue" as heavily Stanislavsky via the Group Theatre—so why not? I went to work to turn the actors into GIs who use words as a casual cover for unwanted emotion in an extreme situation. The actors took to the approach, we were humming along; then came the first preview and the Anti-Defamation League, which issued a proclamation that the play was anti-

Semitic because the central character, a Jew, was neurotic. The author, believing he had written a play against anti-Semitism, refused to change his work. The second preview was cancelled and Mike Gordon returned, unsure though he was which side he was on, and got the curtain raised. The play opened to mixed reviews.

My second play, *Heartsong,* about a marriage that was ruined by an abortion (in 1947!), was produced by a woman who was David O. *(Gone With the Wind)* Selznick's ex-wife and Louis B. (Metro-Goldwyn-Mayer) Mayer's daughter. The play had two directors: Olivia de Havilland's acting coach followed by Audrey Hepburn's husband-to-be Mel Ferrer. It played three cities but never—there is a God—got to Broadway. I began to think about directing.

My next two plays were directed by Harold Clurman, who had been one of the leaders of the Group Theatre, expounding theory to actors like Mike Gordon, my future director. The first play, *The Bird Cage,* starred Melvyn Douglas and featured Maureen Stapleton. In Philadelphia—cursed Philadelphia!—Harold said to Maureen, "Sweetheart, I don't think you know what you're doing in this scene." Maureen answered, "Harold, I don't know what I'm doing in the whole fucking play." The second play, *The Time of the Cuckoo,* was a hit—at last!—starring Shirley Booth. The third day of rehearsal, Shirley walked off the stage, refusing to take direction from Harold. She never changed her mind. I thought more about directing.

Elia Kazan once said Harold Clurman should direct the first three days of any play because no one could explain the socioeconomic-psychological background of the play and the characters more eloquently. After three days, however, Harold should go home. Kazan had begun as an actor in the Group Theatre under Clurman's tutelage. By the time he made that pronouncement, he was the director most in demand, and Clurman was grateful to direct the road company of a play like *A Streetcar Named Desire* which had originally been directed by Kazan.

As a director of plays—not musicals; *Love Life* revealed the musical was decidedly not in his bones—Kazan was arguably the greatest in American theatre history and the creator of the American style of acting—a combination of the Method as practiced by the Group Theatre, technique as practiced by the Theatre Guild, the best of Broadway, and a passion all his own. As a man, he was ruthless and immoral, not above taking out an ad to urge his peers to betray one another to the House Un-American Activities Committee during the McCarthy era. Late in his life, there was an outcry against the proposal that he be given an "honorary" Oscar. Protesters pointed out he had already won two Oscars—one for a film of dubious quality, *Gentlemen's Agreement,* the other for a film of dubious morality and acting that reads as over the top today, *On the Waterfront.* To award another, honoring a man who had destroyed the careers, if not the lives, of peers and friends, was an insult not merely to them and their families but to directors like Alfred Hitchcock who had never even received one Oscar.

There is a long list of artists of distinguished professional achievement and repellent personal behavior. Probably at the top of the list, Wagner and his ardent anti-Semitism. Does behavior lessen achievement? Kazan got his honorary Oscar, but is forever tainted.

Perhaps if, immoral or not, he had directed one of my plays, I would not have begun to think seriously about directing. It was originally more in self-protection of my plays than anything else. I felt I couldn't do worse than the directors I'd had.

I went to every acting class in the city I could and attended the Actors Studio and the Neighborhood Playhouse. I learned most about acting and actors from Stella Adler and Sandy Meisner. Stella was famous for returning from Paris, where she had been studying the Stanislavsky Method with Stanislavsky himself, and announcing to every Method practitioner in the Group, including Clurman, Lee Strasberg, and Kazan: "We're all wrong!"

She was also, and rightly, famous for her courses in Ibsen and Chekhov. The acting method she taught was very similar to Sandy

Meisner's, the most practical teacher of all. His emphasis was on playing an action that shows what the actor wants in the scene. Their influence is apparent today, even in musical theatre.

Why do directors direct? To be in control? To achieve the success they couldn't as actors? To produce theatre that gives the audience an experience only theatre can—moves them, excites and entertains, illuminates, and always makes them want to see more theatre, that's the desired answer. For the director who takes that kind of theatre for granted as his goal, it's imperative to know the answer for everyone, not just his actors, to that most important question in the theatre: why? Why every moment? Why every piece of scenery, every light, every prop, every costume? Why?

It's the most important question in life, too, but who asks it? Not everyone, or at least not everyone expecting an answer. I ask, knowing I don't and won't know all the answers. Some, I guess at; others, I choose to answer my way for myself. Why am I here? I don't ask that. I have no answer; nor does anyone have an answer for me. Why am I gay? That isn't important to me, either; but it was and still is to too many others. Well, I was born gay. Why do I say that? I knew I was when I was seven. How? Sex. At seven? At seven, I knew I was attracted to boys sexually. How did I know? Take my word.

Does it influence me professionally? Not as a director. As a writer? To the same extent that being a Jew does: I often write about outsiders. Do I ever wish I weren't gay? How could I? I would never have had the life I had with Tom Hatcher if I hadn't been gay. What I try to bring to the theatre, both as a writer and as a director, comes from the gifts of that life.

Why did I write this book? The answer is typical: life has no respect for a straight, logical line; it always zigzags. Originally, an editor of a publishing house specializing in theatre books saw the huge pile of notes I had given Sam Mendes for the *Gypsy* he was directing with Bernadette Peters. The editor thought publishing those notes would be extremely informative; display in detail how the process of directing a musical really worked in real theatre life (if that isn't an oxymoron). I set about organizing the notes and providing a background for them, but as I did, the book seemed to be turning more and more into an attack on Sam Mendes, which was far from my intention. I stopped and was ready to quit when Tom stepped in. It wasn't that he didn't want any work to go to waste; rather, he knew he was on the way out and that a book would be something else to keep me busy and get me through the bad part. Why not pass on whatever I knew about directing musical theatre, based on my own experiences? There was a need for something about directing musical theatre—at least I thought so. But knew I was incapable of writing an academic text; inevitably, there would be digressional odds and ends on life and love that would come not only from my experiences directing musicals but from the experiences of my years with Tom.

Tom and theatre, that's what my life has been. And that's what this book is—an effort to say thank you by doing what I can to make the theatre indestructible and to keep Tom alive.

A NOTE ON THE TYPE

This book was set in Adobe Garamond. Designed for the Adobe Corporation by Robert Slimbach, the fonts are based on types first cut by Claude Garamond (c. 1480–1561). Garamond was a pupil of Geoffroy Tory and is believed to have followed the Venetian models, although he introduced a number of important differences, and it is to him that we owe the letter we now know as "old style." He gave to his letters a certain elegance and feeling of movement that won their creator an immediate reputation and the patronage of Francis I of France.

Composed by Creative Graphics, Allentown, Pennsylvania
Printed and bound by R. R. Donnelley, Harrisonburg, Virginia
Book design by Robert C. Olsson